"This book arrived at a time wh[...]_____[...], _____ing business to a different level, and I am 100 percent dedicated to learn new tools and theories. The authentic model is a step-by-step guide to create an executive coaching business. The author tells her personal story in such a way that it captures your attention from the beginning, but she also gives client stories as examples of how to implement the tools. This book contains all the little secrets not only to coach executives but also to understand better what it is that you want and how important it is to work on yourself as well."

Juliana Tabares, author, *One Life to Be You*

"It is like Karaba has become your private personal coach and is by your side on each step of your journey as you follow your passion and dreams. She assists you with everything you need to know on your way to becoming a top-notch leader."

Emma Farr Rawlings, PhD, author, *The Divine Child*,
ICF Master Certified Coach

"It's inspiring to know that Donna has built a thriving coaching business and has laid out the key steps in how to do so!"

Kery Knutson, author, *Create Your Healthy Life*

"*Passion Purpose Profit* is a book that give readers permission to pursue their goal of finding meaningful work while balancing work and home life. It is geared toward those who see coaching as that meaningful work, and it offers a program by which to start a coaching practice. The client stories shared throughout marvelously illustrate practical applications and demonstrate how coaching can help people lead authentic lives. Donna provides some of her own journal entries as lessons to be learned while starting your own coaching business."

Robert Karaba, PhD, New Mexico Highlands University

"Donna has lived her successes and that's why her stories ring with power. Some sole proprietors don't realize they put more time into finding clients than actually delivering the service itself. I can see people using these principles in their own business to find clarity and wisdom from the nitty-gritty, daily mode of operations, to the motivational juice necessary to cope with everyday challenges. Being an entrepreneur, I was inspired to take action immediately on principles delivered in this substance-laden book."

Rainbow, psychic protection instructor, BearAndRainbow.com

"*Passion Purpose Profit* was an enjoyable read. I liked the practicality of the book clearly laying out steps for the process of starting your own coaching career. Donna Karaba's willingness to share from her personal experience especially speaks to me. The best part of the book is that the author is clearly a truly caring person who honestly wants to be of help to others. She sincerely believes tapping into your passion and making it work for you is the best way to go about it. Her willingness to share the obstacles she has overcome, both professionally and personally, is a testament to a remarkable woman."

Erin Cencula, youth minister

"If you are an aspiring coach seeking a path to success while balancing work and family priorities, *Passion Purpose Profit* provides you a clear roadmap. Donna Karaba shares her experience coaching executives by providing stories with each lesson, along with tools and techniques to help you discover your own authentic leadership style. I am inspired by this authentic leadership business model spelled out in this book. A great read for coaches, leaders and parents."

Kate LaBrosse, author, *This Is Me, Bipolar-Free*

"If you are thinking of starting your coaching business and don't know the first steps to take for success, this is a must read! Karaba provides the blueprint through her narratives, tips and downloadable resources. She gives lots of examples of how to coach and how to create your business from the ground up."

Annette D. Matthies, CEO, Aspen Edge Consulting

"Shake free your chains of corporate life and find your passion in executive coaching!"

Alice Barczak, CEO, BeautyCommunity.com

"Finding life balance as a working mother is a challenge, and this book found a way to integrate entrepreneurship and family life!"

Heather Brown, author, *The Diamond Advantage*

"Donna's life journey and quest for a purpose-driven career are an inspiration to anyone that struggles to find the proper work-life balance. Irrespective of your educational background, degree, career-path, or aspirations, *Passion Purpose Profit* shares insights that help the reader ultimately arrive at their personal destination. It is an easy read that lays out a detailed plan that can be used for any type of career, regardless of your vocation."

Chuck Deskins, CEO, Growth Access

"I found this book filled with new information that reinforced and renewed my coaching abilities. I have reviewed my mission, vision and values. I am always motivated for change, and this book reminded me to keep updating and define my goals once again. I recommend it to anyone who needs to be motivated for change or simply needs to be re-connected to one's passion."

Helene Pfeffer, Santa Fe artist, art therapist and art instructor

"Donna Karaba helps leaders become real leaders. She cares about the individual's future and is sincere. She helps rugged individualists get a better handle on their people skills—the soft side. She teaches them how to understand first and ask versus tell, so that they can communicate better, listen better, negotiate win-wins better and be more understanding and empathetic."

Dan Baker, CEO and President, Baker Concrete Construction

"I think Karaba is a magician! The change she drove in our executive was incredible."

Steve Berberich, CEO, California ISO

"The results Donna achieves are greatly needed. Consider me a champion of her work!"

Brenda Thomas, Vice President, Human Resources, California ISO

"Donna's consistent professionalism let me know I would be 'safe' in talking with her. She has very strong listening skills."

Brenda Cavanaugh, SunVIP, Sun Microsystems

"I trusted Donna immediately; she not only provided great direction, she guided me through some major changes in both my professional and personal life. I am much more self-aware."

Rob Davis, Vice President, Great American Financial Resources

Passion Purpose Profit

Table of Contents

Introduction

"Self-actualizing people are those who have come to a high level of maturation, health and self-fulfillment... the values that self-actualizers appreciate include truth, creativity, beauty, goodness, wholeness, aliveness, uniqueness, justice, simplicity, and self-sufficiency."
– Abraham Maslow

Calling as a Career

Inspired by Abraham Maslow, the concept of self-actualization, Marsha Sinetar's book "Do What You Love, The Money Will Follow," and my mentors in life, I decided to trust my heart and follow my passion to coach others. I was determined to prove that this theory could work in my life before I taught others. Unless I was able to experience self-actualization myself, I could not possibly encourage others to do so as a professional coach. The process took many years and several risks, but I can say most assuredly that the effort paid off. I am doing what I love, and the money did follow. I have been able to support my family and their passions and am eternally grateful!

You have been successful thus far in life and now that you have a child your perspective has shifted dramatically. Your roles and identity have changed.

You must decide how you define your role as a parent. How do you envision yourself in this new role? How do you stay in alignment with your values? What kind of career do you long for? You may be successful in a job, but what about your dream to be an entrepreneur? Can you make a living on your own? Can you be true to yourself and experience wholeness, aliveness, and personal freedom? Can you spend the time you desire with your children at your free will?

You *can* be the parent of your dreams *and* do work you love. You can replace your corporate salary and surpass it with a business you operate from home. You can be happy, make a great living, and have the time to raise your children as you wish.

Years ago, I was impressed by an inspiring speaker, a female CEO coach who humbly started out as a "gopher" and worked her way up to teaching executive presence, mustering the courage to demand $7500 a day and getting it. I was inspired by her courage and honesty. Years later, I found through executive coach interviews that I had the right qualifications and courage to make a big impact as an executive coach. I spoke to several executive coaches with large incomes, much more than I had made in my corporate jobs. I then decided to start talking to CEOs in my area as an executive coach.

You can too. Coaching is the easiest "work" I have ever done because coaching comes so naturally. You literally *can* be yourself and do great work. In the chapters that follow, you will learn the process I developed and refined for over ten years. Once I decided on my niche working as an executive coach teaching authentic leadership to CEOs, I was able to bring in over a million dollars in revenue over the years working part time hours. Granted, there were many hours of hard work to build the business, but the majority of the work was enjoyable and I *never* dreaded Mondays. I was excited to have the opportunity to do this kind of work and be well compensated for it.

I am opening my doors to my business so you can step inside and see how it works. I can guide you along the way, as you cross to this side of the river where dreams come true.

You will learn what works in the executive environment. You will also become the parent you dream of being through a career that is meaningful and can be done around your children's schedules. You will inspire others as a role model for entrepreneurship and happy parenting. You may be the only person they know who has followed your passion and made a nice living, while enjoying critical time with your children. You will experience the thrill of managing your own time and having the freedom to be yourself developing your product – *you*. If you have the vision, courage, drive, and determination to take consistent action, you can make your dreams come true.

Chapter 1:

Stuck in a Cycle

"And the day came when the risk to remain tight in a bud was more painful than the risk it took to blossom."
– Elizabeth Appell

Building a Prison and Busting Out

A significant catalyst in my search for self, sprang from a tragic loss at age twenty-one in March of 1983. It was my senior year of college. I could feel the "real world" approaching fast. I had no idea how real life was about to get. With a phone call, I received devastating news. My parents were dead from a "murder suicide" – a terrible label pinned on my loving parents. It was a catastrophic result of mental illness my father had struggled with during my college years.

chased our dream home and had our second child Cole. My job was clearly in jeopardy as both a remote employee and a mother of two. Even though my boss had given me a stellar review, my position was about to move back to headquarters with or without me. My boss asked me how I was planning to raise two children and travel worldwide. That same question was going through my mind as well. I certainly did not want to move back to Silicon Valley after my maternity leave. We were happy where we were. I envisioned raising our children in our new dream home.

The final commission plus severance I received allowed me six months to bond with Cole, spend more time with Ty, and figure out what to do next. I knew how horrible it felt handing a baby to a caregiver after only seven weeks. Those torturous days, stuck in the office, separated from my baby, I would not wish on any mother. Even though I managed to negotiate part-time work, I longed to be with Ty. Having to breast pump hiding in a locked office was humiliating, especially when I had to borrow my male colleague's office and worry about leaking through my blouse or spilling breast milk on the desk. With our second child Cole, I knew I needed more time with my baby and find a way to stay home. I was grateful to spend time with my baby Cole at home, able to observe Ty and Cole playing, and sit on the front porch together watching the rain and lightning flash over the foothills. Still, I was very concerned with how I would help provide for our family financially.

To enable me to stay at home, Rob agreed to start a sales agency. Rob pitched the idea to his employer and I wrote the business plan. Rob was willing to train me in the sales process and to help me build the business for a year before starting his master's program. Having the sales agency allowed us to have a flexible schedule working from home. We both volunteered at our children's school lunch hour and I enjoyed taking the kids to and from school. We also took classes while searching for our master's degree programs. One of us could stop work to pick up the children and then prepare dinner midafternoon. We adored our children's school. We had work/life balance and felt as though we were semi-retired. Life was wonderful. We were able to be present for our children in many ways and build our family's dream together. All that was missing was our master's degrees that would lead us to inspiring work.

The company we represented was sold which negatively affected our business. Rob was ready to start his master's degree full time and teach part time. I chose corporate work that would allow financial stability, part-time work from home, and an opportunity to have my master's courses partially paid by my employer. I wanted to keep our dream home and our kids in an ideal elementary school. I also wanted Rob to pursue his passion.

Finally, I found the ideal master's program at Naropa University. I was called in for an interview and, to my surprise and heartbreak, later received a letter that my application was rejected. After yoga during my lunch hour at work, I shared the news through tears with my teacher and friend. I found out then that the program I had applied for was extremely competitive. My yoga teacher's friend had volunteered at a homeless shelter for a year before being accepted. I had failed to mention my volunteer work.

My next plan was to reach a certain income to solve my problems of longing for more time with family. We could go on vacation and spend more quality time together with a more carefree life. After reaching the next income goal, I was no happier as nothing had changed in our lifestyle. We were not taking more vacations. I was feeling less happy, split emotionally and physically with one foot at work and one foot at home with my family.

I longed for more freedom and time with my children. Three days in the office was too much with only two days at home. I was dying on the inside. My boss was not supporting my request for another day at home even though I was willing to give up my office space. She too was a mother, yet she was clearly climbing the corporate ladder and had a nanny at home with her child. My flexible work arrangement was something she inherited.

The soul whispers, speaks, shouts, cries if it must. Listen.

My left hand reached out to open the top left drawer of the desk in my corner office on the second floor of the building in our headquarters' complex. I noticed the familiar grayish white half folded paper copy of a quote stashed underneath my office supplies. I carefully pulled it out, as I had done several times before. I held it with both hands, "out it goes" I thought, "finally." That same paper had sat in that drawer quite a while and every so often I would pull it out, read the quote, reflect on the possibility, and place it back in the drawer so that others would not see it. Why did I feel the need to hide it? I was hiding the fact that I felt so split. I did not feel comfortable with others knowing how unhappy I was at a deeper level as I longed for wholeness. I resonated so deeply with this quote because I was stuck in my current environment and the cyclical running back to corporate for financial safety and security, yet not finding wholeness with each attempt. I stared at the paper and rolled my chair over to the blue recycle bin by the glass door of my office. I held the paper over the plastic can committed to drop it in, but first I had to read it one last time,

"Our deepest fear is not that we are inadequate. Our deepest fear is that we are powerful beyond measure. It is our light, not our darkness that frightens us. We ask ourselves, who am I to be brilliant, gorgeous, talented, fabulous? Actually, who are you not to be? You are a child of God. Your playing small does not serve the world. There is nothing enlightened about shrinking so that

other people won't feel insecure around you. We are all meant to shine, as children do. We were born to manifest the glory of God that is within us. It's not just in some of us; it's in everyone. And as we let our own light shine, we unconsciously give other people permission to do the same. As we are liberated from our own fear, our presence automatically liberates others." – Marianne Williamson (The paper in my office attributed this quote to Nelson Mandela because he used this in his inaugural address.)

I decided to take action and met with the on-site career counselor and began exploring my values and options. I shared my dream to be a life coach, not realizing this was actually a professional field of work. She suggested I become a free agent. The career counselor was also a life coach in addition to the work she did on campus for the company. She urged me to take a coaching class that Saturday.

Just a few days later, I sat in class reading through the binder learning about the coaching philosophy. The coach introduced new ideas that were quite refreshing. I found what I had been searching for – a positive form of psychology. Eureka! My mainstream psychology courses focused on disease, not health. The coaching philosophy focused on human potential and how to help people achieve fulfillment in life. This philosophy matched my desire to self-actualize as Maslow discussed in his Hierarchy of Needs theory. Abraham Maslow had studied accomplished people in the 1960s when he was considering the need for a "height" psychology as opposed to depth psychology. He found that self-actualizing people were most themselves: self-aware, fulfilled, and whole human beings.

During yoga class on the lunch hour at work – the main reason I was able to get through my workday – I overheard a coworker talking about becoming a coach. I followed him out after class and asked him about coaching. He was taking courses through The Coaches Training

Institute for his coach certification and had done his research to find on-site training courses. I immediately signed up.

Rob's department faculty were encouraging him to pursue a PhD. I was emotionally fried, deplete of spirit, and concerned I was once again playing too small and dying on the inside. I felt my soul's flame flickering. I had to get out before it was too late. I decided to leave another cushy corporate job behind. As I sat in my car looking back at the building and the people I left behind, I started to feel a sense of freedom. When I walked in the door of our beautiful dream home, the weight of the whole political situation at work lifted off my shoulders. I felt so light that I could fly. Now that Rob was well on his way, it was my turn.

Chapter 2:

How I Realized Success

"You will either step forward into growth
or you will step back into safety."
– Abraham Maslow

Finding the Buried Treasure.

My dream business…
12/10/02 I have decided I want to be a life coach.
I am taking classes through CTI, the Coaches Training
Institute.

Soon after leaving my last corporate job in 2002, almost twenty years after leaving my first corporate job, I announced to colleagues that I was starting my own coaching business. I received some congratulations and one person on my worldwide team asked me if I would coach her. My first paying client – yes!

1/6/03 Today is exciting because I am meeting with my first "real" client. She is a wonderful person and I am so honored she wants to work with me.

The day I signed a contract with my first client and received my first check was cause for celebration. My business had officially begun.

Client Story: As we began exploring Monica's passion, she began acting on it and expressing it. She had been hiding the passion inside her and it seemingly had nothing to do with her current job. Yet, a few months later after unleashing her passion Monica began to shine more brilliantly and those around her took notice. She was offered a two-level promotion.

When you begin acting upon your passion, you light a fire within you and that fire feeds other aspects of your life. Others begin to notice something different about you, something brighter, more attractive. Stoking your soul's fire absolutely has an impact on all areas of your life.

Our passions are our clues to our purpose in life. We must explore them if we want to answer the question, "Why am I here?" When we begin acting on our passion we begin to glow. People are attracted to our confidence, joy, and personal presence. We become magnetic. There is a law of attraction at work, personal magnetism is real.

Months later, as I was building my coaching practice, one of my clients shared interest in Naropa's transpersonal psychology program. I felt as though the client was talking about *my program*! It was clear to me that I needed to apply for the transpersonal psychology program again. The envy I felt with my client's interest was a sure sign. After applying the first time and getting a rejection letter, I had given up as if it was fate. With renewed interest, I learned that Naropa had begun an online program, which would work perfectly since we were planning on moving to Ohio for Rob's PhD program.

I called the advisor of the transpersonal psychology program at Naropa and *he* started selling *me* on joining the program. What a switch from my first time applying! Naropa now *wanted* me in their program? I applied, this time including my volunteer work, and was accepted. Finally I was able to enter a master's degree program that suited my interests perfectly. I fell in love with Naropa, meditation practice and classes, the faculty, the curriculum, the students, everything! That entire year of meditation training transformed my life. I had many "peak" experiences that are difficult to describe. Meditation practice has many benefits including unique experiences of interconnection.

We sold our dream house in Fort Collins, CO in a wonderful neighborhood. My best friend lived two houses down. Ty and Cole spent summer nights rounding up friends for "ghost in the graveyard" in our front yard until after dark. They loved both their school and their friends. It broke my heart pulling our sons out of such an amazing environment and saying goodbye to my best friend in tears as we drove away. We had to follow our hearts and continue to pursue the dream of finding meaningful work.

Rob had chosen a PhD program at our alma mater and I chose to obtain my master's degree online at Naropa. We reduced our expenses by $4,500 a month by renting a 70-year-old home on College Avenue in Oxford, OH for $800 per month and placing our sons in public school. The home was a quaint brick home with a small yard and front porch. One day, riding my bike in the rain, I experienced pure joy, feeling so happy and free. The burden from the ball and chain mortgage was gone.

I had taken time out from the business world, thinking that I would never go back. Immersed in school and working with coaching clients, I was detoxing from all the drama I had allowed myself to get caught up in at work at the last corporate job. I also began developing myself spiritually as a coach, developing my intuition through meditation, reading, and writing material that caused me to dig deep emotionally.

I was supported by teachers that were spiritually grounded and giving. It was a highly nurturing time for me. Entering the transpersonal psychology program allowed me the space to fully experiment with self-care and trust in the universe.

After about a month into the program developing a meditation practice, I got up from my desk to walk over to my son's school just a few blocks away. I walked down the front steps turned left down the sidewalk and suddenly stopped in awe. A giant leaf floated down ever so slowly in front of me. It was as if time had slowed down dramatically. I was experiencing a moment caught in a time warp. I had not had an experience like this and realized meditation was altering my perception and experience of reality. I was blown away by the beauty of this one leaf floating as if someone turned the dial of time way down. The leaf seemed to be the only thing happening in the universe. I continued walking and noticed the fragrant flowers along the fence, stopping to plant my face in them, soaking up the beautiful aroma.

6/21/05 It has become a spiritual path. I feel I am on the right one, hoping I find a livelihood along the way.

I put the word out in the town's paper where I was interviewed about my coaching services. The article in the paper helped spur some calls and I started adding clients to my practice.

One day, I walked out onto the porch to retrieve the mail. I held in my hand several envelopes from clients. Each one I opened revealed a check for coaching. I was so overwhelmed with emotion I thought I might jump out of my skin with pure joy. I ran upstairs to the shower to soak up the moment and calm down. I stood in the shower and literally saw stardust, feeling as though the universe had just smacked me with a giant kiss. I was bursting with happiness. Multiple people were paying me to coach them!

As a member of the International Coach Federation (ICF), I reviewed recent survey results, and found that leaders were the primary audience in need of coaching. Reviewing my current clientele, I found that I was already coaching several leaders. I then began to study leadership. I also decided to join a board in order to find more clients as one coach had suggested.

I called on a local non-profit, one I had considered working in during my undergrad days. Now, twenty years later, living back in my college town, I had a second opportunity to support this amazing non-profit by seeking a board position. I could build a community network that might lead to coaching clients. I set up a meeting with the executive director.

I waited downstairs in the quaint College Avenue home that was converted into an office building. A staff member escorted me upstairs. As I was being introduced, the director, Cynthia, dark blonde in her mid-forties, greeted me warmly as she looked up from her desk where she sat looking over a presentation. She stood up and led me to a chair and then sat down across from me. I began sharing my intention for our meeting and handed her my brochure. It was surreal asking her if I could serve on her board, considering my desire to work in the same center as an undergraduate psychology student twenty years prior. We discussed my work and what she was looking for in a board member.

The conversation seemed to be going well until I noticed an odd expression on her face; perhaps she had made her decision. We finished talking, and she walked me to her office door. As I made my exit, I felt a bit awkward about how the interview went.

Shortly after I got back home to my office just down the street, I received an email from her. She thanked me for meeting with her and said she wasn't sure if it was appropriate to ask me during our meeting since I was looking to be on the board, but would I be interested in coaching her? Yes!

Later, Cynthia told me that she was reviewing a presentation by a coach she had seen speak at a recent conference in Columbus as I walked into her office the day we met. Even more coincidental was that I knew the speaker whose presentation was open on her desk. He was a coach from my coaching group in Colorado. She was literally looking for a coach when I stepped into her office. Pure synchronicity!

Cynthia proposed to her board that they hire me to be her life coach. They did! This was my first taste of steady checks from a client that were coming from their business, not their personal checkbook. No need to chase down the payments; the checks came in on time every month. I was thrilled to work with her. She became my ideal client. She not only had a huge following at work, she also had a huge following in the community after a twenty-year stellar career.

My next client was a fellow colleague at school who hired me as his leadership coach. He told me he used that title to sell his partner on allowing him to hire me to coach him. My client was concerned that his business partner would not approve of a life coach and would support a leadership coach.

Next, I created an authentic leadership program that I delivered through Miami University's continuing education program. I borrowed the title from Naropa's program (which I hadn't taken), loving the word authentic combined with my new field of study: leadership. Eventually I did take the Authentic Leadership program in my second year and found that the program I had developed was quite similar, as it had both coaching and meditation tools as key components.

6/23/05 My certainty is growing. I am going to start at the top calling on CEOs and SVPs and get to know some that are interested in developing this form of leadership within themselves, or within their organization.

6/25/05 I witness myself playing as I experience a newfound sense of joy and freedom.

Saturday morning. Stepping into the hallway she looked in on her boys, both curled in their separate beds, sound asleep. She wanted to hear the birds and feel the morning air. Quietly, with Rob and the boys sleeping in, she opened the door and headed out to the park. Sun shining, she was happy to be alive, happy to be among others greeting the new day. Feeling completely free, she walked around the whole park. A line of sprinklers watered the grass, reminding her of her childhood days, running through sprinklers in her backyard having fun with her friends. She felt a sense of mischief as she walked through the puddles, skimming her feet along the top. She ran barefoot in the grass under the spray as the sprinkler rotated. Head up, arms wide, she felt the cool spray on her face and watched the rainbow move along the spray. She ran back and forth squishing her toes through sopping wet muddy grass. A full rainbow touched each side of the ground in front of her. How long had she been playing, she wondered? Her kids would be waking up soon. She put her socks and shoes on quickly and began running home in her drenched clothes, locks of wet hair flowing. She felt like flying. Home again and just 9:19am, could have been an eternity, just an hour or so. Life is good!

7/4/07 I am now an executive coach! So far this year I have booked $108K in business which was the exact goal I set for this year and it is only July! I am very happy now that life is working out well in all areas. I am doing work I truly enjoy. My clients are making great progress. Rob finished his PhD and we are moving to California to another college town for Rob to work at the university. Cole is helping us pack. Ty is at Northwestern, lucky guy.

I found a clear sense of self as I discovered my calling. I was able to bring my spiritual being into my work in the material world. I always felt too spiritual and too artsy for the material world. After all the searching, I finally found my true path. With so much needless suffering in the world, my mission became one that helped free people to be happy in work and in life and help them become more fully present. I discovered my passion and a way to live my life with greater purpose.

Chapter 3:

The Master Key – Awareness Forms Foundation

Keys to Success

"If you can learn to make the mind still, it will be the greatest help to the world."
– Ajahn Chah

The heart of my Executive Coaching program is the Authentic Leadership Business Model™. The underlying force here is authenticity: drawing it forth in yourself, your clients, and in all your business relationships. We begin with the master key component – awareness. By enhancing awareness one can develop emotional intelligence (EI), a crucial ability for leaders. Leaders must be conscious of their emotions, behaviors, and words to be able to choose their responses. In this chapter, you will learn how to develop the awareness that forms the foundation of leadership.

Chapters four through eleven illuminate the remaining keys to the Authentic Leadership Business Model™. I have been refining this model for over a decade. Use these keys to unlock your success, adapting to your clients' needs.

Authentic Leadership Business Model™

A: **A**wareness Forms Foundation

U: **U**nderstand Needs

T: **T**rust by Caring

H: **H**onor Mission and Vision

E: **E**xplore Stakeholder Feedback

N: **N**urture Highest Self

T: **T**each Gaps in Leadership

I: **I**nvestigate ROI

C: **C**ultivate New Business

By utilizing this business model, you will create fertile soil for the seed of your executive coaching business to thrive and blossom.

Why is awareness the foundation? One of the key behaviors needed in leaders is the ability to listen and be fully present to another human being, primarily their staff, as well as their internal and external customers. It sounds easy – you close your mouth and take in what the other person is saying. Pretty simple, right? Hold on, there is a little bit more involved. Consider the many demands on a leader throughout their day. Meeting after meeting, decision after decision. With so much activity, it can be difficult to clear the mind and be present. Ideally the leader can put aside what is pulling from the past or future and become present to the person or situation at hand. Being able to shift gears to listen with an open heart and open mind is a skill that can be developed through mindful practice. Thus, developing a personal mindfulness awareness practice is key for leaders.

Imagine a calm clear lake where you can see all the way to the bottom. The surface, smooth as glass, casts a mirror-like reflection. A calm and clear mind is like the lake. When your mind is clear, unattached, without judgment, and open to what is happening in the present moment, you are ready to listen and be a loving witness able to reflect the truth.

How does one know they are being listened to with someone's full attention?

Personal Story: I remember a day when I was struggling with the decision at the end of my sophomore year in college. I wanted to leave a prestigious university as I was feeling trapped. I needed a fresh start. After talking with my mom, I went into my dad's office in our home to talk with him privately. I told him my reasons for wanting to leave. He sat there looking in my eyes listening to me with his full attention for an hour! I felt his love and compassion. I cried a lot because I knew I was letting him down. Even though he was disappointed, he was willing to support my decision. He clearly had experience listening as an educated clinical psychologist and industrial psychologist. He listened to a lot of people (I know, I typed a lot of his reports), yet our one-on-one experiences were rare.

His ability to listen to me pour out my heart is something I will always treasure. His understanding meant a lot to me. Later, he wrote me a letter to let me know he was proud of me.

Last fall, thirty-five years after my parents' death, my brother gave me a box he had stored in his office. My dad had written thirteen chapters of a book and was negotiating a contract with his publisher in the late 70s. I was so excited to read his writing. I longed to get his guidance in my business. In one chapter on personal development, he mentioned the benefits of meditation.

Mindfulness practice, or meditation, can be explained quite simply. You sit quietly and focus your mind on your breath. Sounds simple enough. And yet, it is one of the most difficult things to put into practice. The challenge is getting in the habit of sitting and paying attention to the breath while also observing the thinking mind without judgment or attachment.

As the attention moves from the breath to individual thoughts, you gently guide the attention back to the breath. It is a process of continually letting go. Letting the thoughts pass like clouds in the sky, not allowing the mind to run away with any one thought, but simply noticing the mind thinking and guiding the mind back to paying attention to the breath.

There are countless books discussing the aspects of the mind and related emotions in the body. The aim of mindfulness awareness practice is to tame the mind and manage the emotions. The brain is a complex machine, with a mind that is always thinking. Mindfulness awareness practice develops the ability to choose responses rather than react habitually.

The benefit is being able to call upon a state of calmness at any point throughout the rest of your day. You begin to become more fully present in each moment and time seems to slow down. You can pay attention to emotions as they come and go and calmly observe. It is a superpower to be able to remain calm in a stressful situation. You can begin choosing your responses rather than reacting habitually. Mindfulness practice affects your ability to control your fight or flight reaction, increasing the capacity to calm the amygdala, the primitive part of the brain.

"Between stimulus and response there is a space.
In that space is our power to choose our response.
In our response lies our growth and our freedom."
– Viktor E. Frankl

Daniel Goleman's book, *Emotional Intelligence*, suggests that emotional intelligence is just as important as intellectual intelligence. After reading an article by John Mayer and Peter Salovey in a psychological journal, Daniel Goleman dug into the research. He learned that self-awareness, self-regulation, motivation, empathy, and social skills can be taught. Wisdom has an emotional quotient which is equally if not more important than intellect for leadership ability.

Goleman found that, "helping children improve their self-awareness and confidence, manage their disturbing emotions and impulses, and increase their empathy pays off not just in improved behavior but in measurable academic achievement." Further research into Social Emotional Learning (SEL) has discovered, "improvements in attention and working memory, key functions of the prefrontal cortex. This strongly suggests that neuroplasticity, the shaping of the brain through repeated experience, plays a key role in the benefits from SEL."

Emotional Intelligence has been applied in the business setting with leadership development. Meng, the "Jolly Good Fellow" at Google developed a popular seven-week course and book entitled, "Search Inside Yourself." He teaches emotional intelligence using mindfulness practice and good mental habits grounded in the theory of neuroplasticity, or "the capacity of the brain to develop and change throughout life." Our brains develop new neural pathways through new life experiences which means we have the capacity to develop new habits and let go of habits that are no longer helpful. Therefore, by learning to be mindful, a person can remain calm where previously they might have acted out in anger, behaving inappropriately or exchanging regrettable words.

In my experience as an executive coach, emotional intelligence is key in leadership capability at the top of the organization. Leaders who are kind and loving have more loyal followings. The main reason a person will leave their job is due to the relationship with their supervisor. Therefore, the more you can help a leader develop a caring relationship with their staff members, the healthier the organization.

As a coach and teacher, I believe it is best to lead by example and develop a mindfulness awareness practice. There are many ways people practice that do not require a sitting practice. Yet, I have found that a sitting practice is a very useful discipline to engage in regularly. While being still, you are able to place your full attention on steadying the mind and observe how the mind works. With consistent practice, you become more present in each moment of life. Some people prefer to walk, run, bike, swim, or practice yoga while keeping a focus on what is happening in each moment with each breath. These moving meditations are mindfulness practices. The point of the practice, whether seated or moving, is to pay attention to what is happening in the present moment and be fully there.

Client Story: Brad had an issue with coming across as aggressive in meetings, putting some colleagues in an awkward defensive position. One of my client's peers felt as though they might get into a "backyard brawl." When Brad found out how he was being perceived and realized meditation might help, he asked me to teach him how to meditate. We planned to do this training in our next meeting.

When we met again, he was eager to get started. He suggested we take a walk outside. We walked through the bustling financial district and found a park bench. I explained what we were about to do and guided him in a seated meditation. I began with these instructions, which you may try now.

"Sit in a comfortable position with both feet flat on the ground. Lift your spine tall, sitting upright and not too stiff. Place your hands on your thighs. Cast a soft gaze toward the ground or close your eyes, whichever is more comfortable. Focus your attention on the

breath. Notice the breath as it is. There is no need to control the breath. Just notice the feeling as you inhale and exhale through the nose. Relax your forehead, jaw, and tongue. Pay attention to the breath. Notice the feeling of cool air entering the nostrils as you breathe in and warm air exiting the nostrils as you breathe out. If your mind wanders gently bring your attention back to the breath. Observe your thoughts as they float by like clouds in the sky. If you find yourself thinking, label this activity as "thinking" and come back to the breath. Continue observing and letting go of thoughts, refocusing the mind and your attention on the breath. I will be silent now for two minutes so that you can practice on your own. (Two minutes of silence.) Observe whether your mind wandered during this time. Without any judgment, gently guide your attention to the breath, inhaling and exhaling. Continue focusing on the breath allowing thoughts to float by, you can come back to those thoughts later once we are done practicing. Focus the mind on the breath, inhaling and exhaling through the nose. Now, gently open your eyes."

After practicing, we discussed how meditation works and how he could practice this at home, working up to ten minutes a day. As we began future meetings together, we started by meditating together for about ten minutes with some portion guided and some silent, similar to the instructions here.

Brad began practicing at home by relaxing on his patio each night after work. One day he called, excited to share what had just happened during a meeting. He was meeting with a colleague that previously would have turned into a contentious interaction, yet this time, he noticed that he was relaxed and calm, focused *on listening to his colleague instead. Brad was sitting back in his chair aware of his body. As the meeting came to an end, his colleague thanked him for listening.*

Brad was ecstatic to be able to monitor his own emotions and body language. This was a huge shift. He went from zero self-awareness to "practically floating above my body able to control my words and emotions and listen to my colleague with my full attention." He was also noticing many shifts in his ability to be fully present with both family members and colleagues. That was exactly the result we were going for. Yahoo!

Begin developing your own practice in mindfulness. You can use this form of meditation by following my simple instructions. You may want to start small with two minutes of silence and work your way up to ten minutes a day. That is all you need. If you prefer to lengthen the time to 20 or 30 minutes, you may find you enjoy a longer practice. Do not be hard on yourself if you forget to practice, just get back to developing a habit. Some people have a special place in their home or office to sit and meditate. Others practice while waiting for their tea to brew. I prefer to sit first thing in the morning from ten to twenty minutes or longer. Find a time and a place that works for you.

I have found it is helpful to provide guided meditation to students who are new to the practice. Too many minutes of silence can be difficult for someone who is just starting out with a mindfulness practice. You can offer a simple mindful start to your meeting. This will bring your client into the present moment and help them learn how to let go of everything that has happened earlier in the day and everything that is planned for after your meeting. As you coach your clients, you want them to be fully present. By starting with a mindful awareness practice to begin your meeting, you will bring your client and yourself more into the present moment. By being fully present you increase the likelihood of a productive coaching session.

If your client is eager to develop a personal practice, you may want to offer ideas based on the client's needs, whether they are ready for a silent meditation, or if they prefer a written meditation to recite or memorize to maintain their focus. Some people may choose a mantra or a word such as love, or simply say to themselves, "I breathe in, I breathe out." Others may prefer listening to a guided meditation.

Student Story: Sandra preferred being guided during meditation and was uncomfortable with the silence. As I guided her with a simple meditation, I repeated a set of lines, an excerpt from a book on meditation. She asked if she could take home a copy of the meditation I had shared in class. Sandra was struggling with the responsibility of caring for her mother whose health was declining. Sandra practiced at home using the written meditation and memorized it. At our next meeting, through tears she shared how grateful she was to be practicing this technique. She noticed feeling more relaxed and rejuvenated and how this affected her relationship with her mother. She had not realized how much stress she was holding in her body caring for her mother.

As you cultivate awareness in your own life you become more grounded, more intuitive, and more present for your clients. It is also important for your client to develop these same qualities to become a more mindful leader. Start your meetings with an awareness exercise and see the difference it makes to the quality of the meeting and the outcome for your clients.

Chapter 4:

Key 2 – Understand Needs

"We think we listen, but very rarely do we listen with real
understanding, true empathy. Yet listening, of this very special
kind, is one of the most potent forces for change that I know."
– Carl Rogers

U nderstanding the needs of your clients is crucial to your ability to provide value. I have spent thirty-five years focused on
listening for and responding to client needs. On one mem-
orable occasion after landing a worldwide marketing job at the headquarters of a Fortune 500 semiconductor company, my colleague,
assigned as my "buddy," helped me get adjusted. He cleaned out a
section of his filing cabinet and handed me a box of files. He was especially happy to be handing over one particular account. They were,
according to him, the biggest "pain in the neck" and "so demanding."
As I picked up the box, grateful for the accounts, he said "Good luck!"

Over the years, this account became our number one account, beating out IBM. I loved working with this customer because they treated us like business partners. I always knew what they needed because we had a close relationship with consistent meetings where they were quite vocal. Back at headquarters, I only had to mention the account name and any one of the 350 people in our division would drop what they were doing to help. I became my company's worldwide sales manager and let go of my other accounts. I visited all my client's locations worldwide. It was the job I dreamed of back in college, traveling the world as a business woman. I had arrived.

It *was* a dream job until it turned into a nightmare on day nine of a ten-day trip to Europe. I literally was staying in a castle in Ireland and found myself calling home crying, looking for permission to leave. I wanted to be at home with my family. I sorely missed our two-year-old son. Obviously, I had no idea this might happen when I planned the trip. My husband listened to my heartache and gave me the permission I needed. I left the meeting a day early.

What I *had* gained from this job was an understanding of how to satisfy the needs of my customers by *listening* to their needs. I also learned an important lesson in paying attention to my emotional needs and what I could and could not sign up for now that I was a mother. You too may find this tug and pull in your various roles. It is important to listen to your heart and ensure you understand your own needs. Remember that you cannot effectively serve others if your needs have not been met first.

Understanding the needs of your client will drive the activity of the business and will set the course for your service offerings and product development. As a business owner and sole proprietor, remember to balance the needs of your customers with your own needs. Be careful not to give more than the client is giving. One famous psychologist and family therapist advised, "never go more than half way." If you do, it may take a toll on your health. Be sure your client is equally engaged in the coaching process. Be careful not to serve too much. Because you love making people happy, you are a natural born listener – and what better way to make people happy than giving them what they want? Probe with open-ended, powerful questions and then remain quiet. Give them your full attention as they tell you what they need. There is a saying often used in sales training and that is, "You have two ears and one mouth – use them in that proportion." This is a good reminder. Learn about your client and understand their needs by listening.

You must care about your client's business success as if you are their business partner. You are even more valuable than a business partner because you can be objective and allow your client to think and plan openly unguarded.

Later in chapter seven, we discuss key stakeholder 360-degree feedback. By listening to people who surround your client as superiors, peers, direct reports, and customers, you can gain a broad perspective to assist your client in navigating their current environment most successfully. As you obtain a bird's eye view of the landscape where your client lives, you will determine what will help them advance their ability to lead most effectively. Your client company stakeholders will tell you what they need when you inquire with genuine interest. Your client will also share their needs with you. Listen, honor their wisdom, and help your client hear what they are saying. Through inquiry and dialogue, those areas that are most important to your client will naturally surface. From here, you can assist your client in developing an action plan to reach their goals.

The skill of listening requires empathy and suspended judgment. By continuing to build a consistent mindfulness awareness practice, you will learn to let go of thoughts and release judgment, becoming more fully present in each moment. Hold an intention to understand your client while maintaining an open mind and a loving heart. Similar to the calm surface of the lake that reflects the beauty of the landscape, you can be that mirror for your clients.

Partner with your client to understand their business goals so that you can do your work with clarity. It is helpful to understand the context in which you are working and what is at stake for a successful outcome. Here are some questions to ask key stakeholders before you begin the coaching assignment to understand your client's business goals:

1. What is the reason you are hiring me to coach this candidate? e.g. To develop a high potential leader to succeed senior executives; executive is leading a key initiative worth $200M and has developed relationships with internal and external customers who are key stakeholders in this important project; this project has significant implications for the company's viability.

2. How will we know that this coaching engagement has been successful? e.g. The executive will demonstrate strategic thinking and inspire his team with a clear vision. The project will be implemented on time with the executive gaining necessary approvals.

3. What is the worst thing that can happen if the candidate does not receive coaching? e.g. We lose a loyal employee with the knowledge and expertise developed over the last fifteen years; we lose opportunity costs of the relationships tied to a $50M project; we damage relationships tied to the project and experience project delays.

4. If we are successful with the outcomes defined, what is the bottom-line result of coaching this leader? e.g. Savings on executive recruitment and replacement plus the value in maintaining key relationships tied to the project with a monetary value of $500K.

There are four reasons to establish clarity on the deliverables: 1) to quantify the potential value your coaching will bring the client company before you quote your service offerings and retainer fee, 2) to ensure you complete a successful engagement, 3) to determine the ROI and what impact your work can have on the client company who is funding your work, and 4) to obtain a client testimonial and reference for marketing purposes in securing new business.

To complete a successful coaching engagement with your client company, understand key stakeholders needs and expectations as well as the potential gains the company will receive in realizing coaching candidate goals. You can determine the value of a successful engagement by calculating the return on the investment.

Client Story: I asked the following questions to Larry, COO and direct report to the CEO of a multibillion-dollar company. I wanted to determine the value and client expectations of the assignment:

1. What are the reasons you are hiring me to coach you?

    I am in charge of a key project and need help as I cope with some devastating personal issues. I need to increase my self-confidence to obtain board approval for various stages of funding so that my team can complete the assignment.

2. How will we know this coaching engagement is successful?

    Success will include my staff being on board and excited about the project, the board has approved necessary funding, I am happier and more confident, and we are on path to realize this dream project.

3. What is the worst thing that can happen if you do not seek coaching?

    My personal life issues will detract from my ability to be effective at work. I will fail to meet essential milestones to manifest this high-profile assignment and vision for the company. I could lose my job, not have the opportunity to realize this dream, and disappoint my team who is inspired to be here because of this exciting opportunity.

The best way to build an executive coaching business is by doing great work at the top of the organization with the Chief Executive Officer directly. Indirect relationships are more challenging, yet still offer opportunities to impact leaders who have great influence.

- Understand the reason your client wants to hire you and define the specific goals and outcomes your client expects from your work together.

- Understand the costs to your client if they do not fix this problem or miss an opportunity. Place a value on the problem or opportunity to the best of your ability by researching this on your own, adding any data your client can provide. Business owners are responsible for their bottom line, so it behooves you to know your value to the company and be in a position equipped to review the ROI at the close of the assignment with the CEO or other key stakeholder.

By understanding the needs of your client, you can offer your services at a worthy price knowing the value you are providing is at least tenfold. I prefer a simple annual retainer to allow me freedom to provide excellent value to my clients. Discuss with your client the cost of not solving this problem. Determine how much value you will bring the company by solving this problem. At the end of the assignment, review the estimated ROI to the actual ROI to understand how much the company gained realizing the coaching objectives. This offers you the opportunity to understand your own value as it relates to the clients' needs and their overall success.

Chapter 5:

Key 3 – Trust through Caring

"Let us be grateful to people who make us happy, they are the charming gardeners who make our souls blossom."
– Marcel Proust

B ased on your coaching education thus far, you recognize that coaching is not just a career, it is your calling. You have many natural talents that create trust and lasting relationships. Your ability to care for others and empathize with their situation is a quality typically found in a family member or close friend. Your care extends beyond most because you care about human suffering and human happiness. You can meet strangers and establish trust and rapport quickly. Your curiosity enables you to relate well with people. You are imaginative and creative. You have an artistic eye that permits you to see possibilities that others do not see for themselves. Your genuine care creates trust with your clients immediately. A trusting relationship allows for powerful inquiry and dialogue to deepen the conversation. You build trust naturally through a combination of qualities that demonstrate genuine caring.

Do not take your abilities lightly. Too often we negate our natural talents and skills because we have not had to work hard to obtain them. Even Einstein said, "I have no special talent. I am only passionately curious." He also said, "The true sign of intelligence is not knowledge but imagination." We will likely agree that Einstein was quite gifted using both curiosity and imagination to create great value to society.

How much knowledge, curiosity and imagination do you need to coach executives? As I was formulating the plan to coach CEOs, I interviewed executive coaches in the nearby metropolitan area. One executive coach shared, "People care more about how much you care than how much you know." I often come back to these wise words and remind myself to relax and not waste time over-preparing. Remember that your ability to care *is* valuable. Care is often demonstrated through curiosity.

CEOs are people who rarely have an impartial ear where they can speak openly. The freedom to be vulnerable is not an option for CEOs because those close to them are either a board member, peer, staff, or family member and each has a stake in the matter. Your trust and care are valuable. You are not only a confidant, but often a strategic thinking partner who is able to offer exceptional insights. Because you care about your client's happiness, you can provide a safe space, impartial ear, and an open mind that allows your client to think clearly without concern for other peoples' agendas. Your client can be free to express their true potential. (Note: When I say CEO, please understand this same authentic leadership model works for direct reports and rising stars, people in positions you are also likely to coach.)

People are focused on their own problems and if you demonstrate genuine care in helping them solve their problems, then you will build trust which opens the door for their soul, their higher self, to come out to play. You can then be that midwife of sorts, nurturing that seed within them that has been there all along, perhaps starved to the point it is hard for them to see or feel, but nevertheless it is there to be nurtured with care. As you recognize passion and nurture that passion, your client's passion grows, and your client begins to blossom.

Trust is a key factor in the success of the coaching engagement and it is your job to establish trust. Pay attention to your intuition – what your gut is telling you – when you interview the coaching candidate and when you are working together. You will find that some clients may not be willing to do the necessary work to make a change, or they have a personal issue that gets in the way of you doing your work. You will not mesh perfectly with every client. There must be good synergy between you, and mutual respect. If at any point you find trust is broken, you must find a way to establish trust or end the relationship. Perhaps you are not the right coach for this client, or you are, and you merely need to speak up.

Client Story: I caught James in a lie after he called to cancel his appointment at the last minute. It was not the first time he had to cancel or leave abruptly. This time I found out he had made up an excuse. I had to get to the bottom of this, or let this client go. I could not continue working with someone I did not trust. I considered what happened and how I felt. I decided to confront James to inquire about his story and tell him what I had learned. I gave him the ultimatum to be open and honest or we would need to end the coaching engagement.

He admitted he had lied to get out of our meeting that day. He apologized profusely and explained that he was very anxious in intimate 1:1 relationships and meetings due to a childhood trauma and was working with a therapist on the issue. In contrast, he could speak to large groups effortlessly with a wonderful sense of humor. He assured me that he would be honest going forward and absolutely wanted to continue working together.

The conversation allowed us to deepen the relationship. By pressing the pause button to handle this issue and clear the air we were able to establish two-way trust. We then moved forward in a more genuine and real way. At the end of our assignment, James gave me an hour and fifteen minutes of honest, stellar feedback stating that he trusted me implicitly from the first day we met.

It is imperative to have a trusting relationship for a successful coaching engagement. Sometimes you must take a hard line with a client because you care. You owe it to your client to create a safe space and this can take time. You know, perhaps better than your client, that trust is essential for the client to be a more effective leader. At any given moment, you may need to press the pause button and ask tough questions. Your gut, your intuition, acts like an honesty gauge, so pay attention to how you feel and respond accordingly.

Even though I knew I might lose a client by calling him out and giving him an ultimatum, it turned out to be necessary for the client's growth. If there is ever a question of trust due to a client's unusual behavior such as showing up late, leaving early, or cancelling, do not shy away from confrontation. Check in with your client to see what is really going on. Be open and courageous always; your client's ability to grow requires *your* honesty!

Student Story: In a group coaching class, I had noticed Anna was not participating in our large group discussion. Her written assignments were brilliant, and I wanted her to share her powerful insights with the group. I could not understand why she was not engaging in dialogue with the rest of the group. I provided both large and small group exercises breaking the group up into dyads and triads.

As I observed the small group dialogues, I noticed Anna shar-
ing in the small group discussions. I found a moment to ask her
privately why she was not speaking up more in the larger group. She
informed me that she is an introvert and is much more comfortable
in small group discussions where she can more safely engage in dia-
logue. She explained that she needs to process a question internally
before offering her thoughts to a large group. She needs time to
think things through before speaking. In the large group, she will
acquiesce to the extroverts who tend to jump right in and steal the
floor before she has had a chance to process the question.

I learned an important lesson following my curiosity. That is,
I had not created a safe environment for her to speak to the larger
group. She taught me that to engage her in dialogue, she would
prefer to be offered quiet time to consider her answer in writing.
With time to process her thoughts on paper first, she could then
share her input with the larger group. I thus began instructing
the group with Anna's needs in mind, allowing time for students
to consider the question by providing silent time for writing. The
class discussion was richer with everyone engaging in dialogue. I
was so pleased we found a way to include her intellectual content
with the class. Anna's feedback was very valuable and changed
the way I led group discussions.

You are venturing into a helping profession. The most important
thing you can do is to be in service to another human being's growth by
developing and offering your full presence with love in your heart. Being
a coach is an honorable role. Your client is trusting you with their soul,
exposing their heart and their vulnerability. Treat your client with the
same loving care you would offer your child. By becoming a conduit of
love, you can hold the sacred space required for your client's profound
experience of self-realization and actualization. Your goal is to facilitate
your client in aligning internally to become an authentic leader.

The Coaching Candidate Intake

To complete a coaching "intake," allow approximately four hours for this initial coaching candidate meeting – longer if your format is an entire day each month.

Imagine you have a meeting with Eric, a Chief Executive Officer of a billion-dollar company who has engaged you to coach him directly. You set up an appointment to meet at an off-site meeting room to be on neutral ground and away from the office environment. You arrive 30 minutes in advance to allow time to gather yourself before the meeting. You take this time to calm your nerves and meditate. You review your agenda and rehearse the meeting in your mind. You enter the building and wait in the lobby to greet your client. You are calm and clear ready to lead the meeting. This first coaching session is intended to develop a personal relationship and get to know your client's needs.

Eric arrives entering the lobby and you greet him with a professional handshake and look him in the eye acknowledging him with enthusiasm. You then escort him to the meeting room. You build trust through professional rapport. You begin a dialogue based on questions you have prepared in advance. You begin by: 1) confirming the reason Eric engaged you as his coach by restating the problem he wants to solve using his words as well as the outcome he shared in your initial conversation, 2) you ask Eric how he wishes to be different based on your coaching, 3) what is his vision for himself personally, professionally, organizationally? and 4) how exactly will you both know if this has been a successful executive coaching engagement?

(Note: You can use a standard questionnaire, or you may choose to adapt your questionnaire for each client. You can build rapport and gain trust with your client by being fully present and going with the flow. Either way, with a structured format or unstructured following your client's lead, your client will appreciate your full attention as you engage authentically.)

Share your ethical code of conduct, and some of the tools you will use today and in future sessions, including the life and leadership wheels, primary focus areas, 360-degree assessment surveys, and evaluations. Review your proposal and gain agreement with Eric's signature. Obtain a list of key stakeholders your client would like you to interview and survey. Provide an overview of the structure of each coaching session and remain open to designing the structure together listening for specific needs and how he prefers you to interact with him as his coach. Does he prefer meeting for a full day once a month, or half day twice a month (this will depend on the distance you need to travel). You also have the option of phone or videoconference. Be open to designing the meeting format. If you have found a format you prefer, simply recommend that format and see if this works for your client.

By clarifying the desired outcome and structure up front, you set your client at ease with your confidence and you demonstrate your professionalism as an executive coach. You want to ensure that you both are clear about what a successful engagement looks like and how you plan to work together.

The client questionnaire provides you with some insight into the legacy your client wishes to leave, his worldview, his strengths and accomplishments, and his unique talents. The leadership wheel exposes gaps or imbalances in your client's executive leadership role and reveals insight into your client's *ideal* leadership role. The wheel of life allows you to take a snapshot of where the client is now and where they envision each area of life in its ideal state. Finally, the primary focus areas highlight the key goals with priority by number and include titles, descriptions, and measurements for success.

By the end of the first meeting – the intake – you should be crystal clear about what a successful client coaching engagement looks like with this client. Your goal is to walk away having completed the primary focus areas, the client questionnaire, the leadership wheel (customized to the leader's goals and objectives), the wheel of life, and detailed current and desired states.

It is a meaningful experience to offer a business leader a trusting relationship where they can share their personal, professional, and organizational issues openly. You can provide your client a safe, confidential, objective business perspective while holding space for them to explore their thoughts, strategies, and goals for themselves and their business. Your ability to impact your client's life and business has a profound ripple effect.

Intake Results:

Leadership Wheel

Once you have built that initial trust with your client Eric, complete the Leadership Wheel. This provides you with a snapshot in time of where Eric is now and where he wishes to be. Using a scale of zero to ten, zero being the center of the wheel, and ten being the perimeter of the wheel, have your client rate each area of their life as a leader. Zero is where it could not be worse and ten is where he sees his leadership style at its best. Eric will then rate each area subjectively and draw a curve in that piece of the pie where that number fits. Take notes to explain the client rating for that category. Once you have your client rate each category using a zero to ten scale, fill out the detailed current and desired states forms so that you both get a clearer idea of where Eric is now and what his vision is for optimal leadership.

Use the Leadership Wheel to help identify Eric's authentic leadership role. This wheel may expose areas he would like to focus on developing and areas where he is inherently strong.

Locate the Leadership Wheel here:
www.karabaconsulting.com/clientforms

Life Wheel

When you meet with Eric, your executive coaching client, it is essential to capture a holistic view of his life. With this perspective, you can work with your client as a whole human being. You need to understand where his life is in balance or out of balance. There is crossover between your client's personal and professional life. The out of balance areas in his personal life are impacting his work life.

Proceed the same way as you did with the Leadership Wheel by now utilizing the Life Wheel. You may assign different names to categories, or split categories as Eric, your client desires.

By using the wheel of life, you can take a snapshot in that first meeting to determine where Eric is currently operating in each area of his life. Even though you are primarily coaching in a segmented area called "career," you need to be aware of what is going on in your client's personal life. Coaching in one area will affect the other areas. Eric will become more effective as a leader by paying closer attention to the areas of his life that need his attention. Eric will also learn new tools and develop new habits to increase his self-awareness. Once you have your client rate each category using a zero to ten scale, fill out the detailed current and desired states forms so that you both get a clearer idea of Eric's ultimate vision.

Locate the Life Wheel here:
www.karabaconsulting.com/clientforms

Student Story: Paul was surprised to find his Life Wheel so out of balance. He had rated his fun and recreation a two. Paul had four children and was the president of a manufacturing company. He was afraid of missing out on his children's lives and was seeking a way to spend more time with his family. He used to golf, but had not golfed in years, yet was surrounded by pictures of golf courses and golf paraphernalia. He teared up as he shared a story of a recent train ride where a mother of four was complaining about her husband who worked all the time. He felt like she was speaking directly to him; the message was loud and clear that Paul was doing the same thing to his wife and kids. I worked with Paul to bring balance into his personal life and make some drastic changes in his work schedule. We began prioritizing fun and recreation and discovering what aspects of his work could be delegated to free up some time. He began taking a more active role going on dates with his wife, and creating 1:1 time with each child. Fortunately, we caught this imbalance in time while his children were still young. He also managed to play a few rounds of golf. Bringing this one aspect of Paul's life back into balance had significant impacts on his relationships at home and at work.

Primary Focus Areas

Finally, complete the Primary Focus Areas, determining what Eric's top goals are for coaching and how you will define each goal with a title, description, and measurement for success.

Set up Coaching Calendar

Determine your next set of coaching appointments and calendar out the entire year through the length of engagement. With the dates preset, it is easy to create a new habit of carving out time for leadership reflection and development. As an example, for one client, I recently lined up in-person appointments the first Wednesday of the month and video conference appointments the third Wednesday of the month. Once these are on the calendar, you can easily plan accordingly and adjust when necessary.

Now you have completed a professional executive coaching intake.

Locate the Primary Focus Areas here:
www.karabaconsulting.com/clientforms

What Is the Typical Format of an Executive Coaching Session?

The typical format for coaching includes a brief check-in at the beginning of the session to review what has happened since the last session. Discuss obstacles that prevented forward action on goals or homework. You can inquire into each obstacle and help the client see what specifically got in the way. Most of the session is devoted to the client's current agenda. Finalize the meeting by reviewing homework assignments or the client's "action plan."

I provide a meeting agenda template to help clients plan our next meeting and a recap form to fill out at the end of the meeting to note the highlights and their homework assignments. I like to have clients send me a copy for my file which helps us both be on the same page. Your client can fill out the agenda for the next session and provide this at the beginning of the meeting or prior to the meeting for your review. This planning activity creates a productive coaching session and ensures the client gets what they intended from the meeting. Not every client you encounter will be inclined to utilize the forms for planning, but it will be helpful to remind your client occasionally that these tools exist. These forms help your client track their own progress and development and create the start of an agenda for the next meeting.

Clients need to do most of the work between coaching sessions for you to have a successful client engagement. The client must be motivated for change. You can assist your client greatly by helping them become aware of their most compelling future. This will pull them forward. It is much more effective to be pulled toward a desirable future than to be motivated by fear.

Client Story: Mark learned through his 360-degree feedback that when he walked from his office to a meeting, he ignored his staff. He had no idea that his staff felt invisible. After some coaching around the topic of employee self-esteem, he and his superior set goals with each other to engage more with staff. A few minutes of conversation with a staff member or simple acknowledgement goes a long way from a leader. Mark learned that leadership requires more being than doing. Being present for others is important for team engagement and providing employees the message that they are valuable to the organization.

Teaching Self-Responsibility

As a leader, a coach, and as a parent, I have encouraged my children and my clients to take self-responsibility in life, to think for themselves, and to trust their own wisdom. I teach the same thing to my clients to empower their staff. There is a story of a staff member walking into his manager's office with a bunch of monkeys on his back. The monkeys represent problems that the staff member is struggling with. The staff member tries to hand his manager the monkeys one by one. The manager has a choice of taking the monkeys off his employee's back, or helping the employee think about the options available to get the monkeys off their back. In other words, I teach my client to coach their employees through inquiry, dialogue and deep listening and allow the employees to rely on their own wisdom in resolving the monkey issue. It is helpful to have a boss who you can run ideas past and who will coach you to the answer inside yourself. Ultimately, leaders need to make their own decisions, yet it is helpful to be able to talk things out with another leader who can be mindfully present.

Quarterly Evaluations

Check in every quarter with your client to ensure the primary focus areas are up-to-date. If anything has changed, this is a good opportunity to get back on the same page by revising this list. Survey client behavior shifts with stakeholders and update key stakeholders on your client's progress. Updates may be done monthly if several stakeholders are involved. Discuss specific needs with the primary stakeholder.

Celebrate Successes

Each time your client has a breakthrough, celebrate the success. Applaud their effort. Acknowledge the fact that it takes courage and focused effort to change. Remind your client to reward their successful behavior with an item from their self-care list or something creative to mark this achievement. Success breeds success.

Utilizing your natural abilities and talents combined with a professional intake you have built a solid foundation of trust to provide your client an optimal environment to become an authentic leader.

Chapter 6:

Key 4 – Honor Mission and Vision

"Everyone has his own specific vocation or mission in life;
everyone must carry out a concrete assignment that demands
fulfillment. Therein he cannot be replaced, nor can his life
be repeated, thus, everyone's task is unique as his specific
opportunity to implement it."
– Viktor E. Frankl

My hope is that you identify and work with your ideal clients. Take note of your client portfolio and identify these ideal clients. What is their mission, vision, and values? Do your research to determine if your prospect's mission and vision is in alignment with your values. Can you work with this client? Is this prospect in line with your ideal client profile? Focus your efforts.

After closing new business, meet with the key stakeholders to ensure you understand their mission and vision as well as their expectations for a successful engagement. Often, stakeholders include the chief executive officer, chief operating officer, or VP of human resources depending on the coaching candidate's position in the company. You need to determine what each stakeholder expects for a successful outcome for this coaching candidate and who will participate in progress updates. Who are the key stakeholders involved in your coaching candidate's success? It is important to ensure you deliver upon expectations of each stakeholder and manage these expectations with periodic updates.

You will find a variety of key stakeholder and client scenarios. You need to understand the context and culture of the organization you and your client are working in. Each client situation is unique, and it is helpful to be armed with information from all perspectives: the client's company, the coaching candidate, and those in their circle of influence.

Client Stakeholder Story: I had reached out to a VP of human resources who shared a particularly challenging situation with an executive who had been blindsided on a personal level. The situation was causing some issues at work in his dealings with staff. She explained why she chose me to coach this executive who reported directly to the CEO. In a separate meeting, I met with the CEO to understand his desire for this executive and why he chose coaching. The CEO understood that this key executive was going through a difficult time personally and was particularly challenged with a highly visible work assignment with key internal and external customer relationships inside and outside the company. The CEO hoped the COO could increase his confidence with the board and empower his staff.

In another similar client scenario, the VP of human resources matched me with a candidate that reported indirectly to the CEO and directly reported to a vice president. I met with all three stakeholders individually. The coaching client had been deal-

ing with significant personal loss and her personal situation was clouding her ability to see that the entire organizational culture had shifted with the new CEO's leadership. As an outsider, it was easy for me to see what had changed in the cultural landscape.

In both cases, each stakeholder provided useful information and direction. Empathy, and compassion were required. I helped both clients navigate the personal and professional realms with a holistic approach. In the first scenario, I helped my client gain the self-confidence he needed to obtain necessary funding approval from the board for a $60M project. In the second scenario, I helped my client shift from an "expert" to a "collaborative" team player and behave more like a member of the executive team. In both cases, the clients stepped more fully into their executive shoes.

Once you have defined the key stakeholders' objectives, it is time to interview the candidate to determine if it is a right fit and to review those objectives along with the coaching candidate's objectives. Clarify their mission and vision using their words. Define the coaching process clearly along with your ethical code of conduct and be sure to make your client aware that this will be an open engagement. The objectives and action plan you both decide upon will be made known to each stakeholder. You will need to find out from the coaching candidate who they wish to include in the 360-degree feedback process.

Client Story: I learned in an engagement with Steve, a chief operating officer, that the 360-degree feedback is an essential component of executive coaching. After securing a new client company, I found out that the coaching candidate had requested that the VP of human resources keep our coaching engagement confidential from his colleagues and staff. I included an optional 360-degree assessment in my contract. There were some private personal issues that likely caused my client's request. For that reason, his request seemed appropriate even though it should have raised a red flag. My ideal client is openly proud to work with me in a coaching capacity. I confirmed with the VP of HR the client's need for confidentiality and had approval which nullified the 360 as "optional." Unfortunately, I did not revise the agreement as it had already been signed and that was not on my mind as much as this client and the challenging situation at hand. It would have been best at that moment to line out the 360 as an option.

With that lesson, I now start with a 360-degree assessment with my executive clients and do not make it optional. It is necessary to work with a client openly in an indirect relationship due to client company funding and multiple stakeholders involved.

Be prepared to compare your ideal client profile to each coaching candidate. Take on assignments that align with your integrity, including being open about your coaching engagement. Do not compromise and assume the client knows best. Stay in your advisory role to ensure you give the best service from start to finish. An open engagement must be non-negotiable in indirect engagements. With each stakeholder having skin in the game, you each help the client succeed and you can openly share the progress of your assignment. Use specific survey results and data points gathered from each stakeholder to maintain open communication with progress updates.

I share my lessons learned with you, so that you will pay attention to the red flags and make wise decisions to either insist on an open engagement or walk away. Not only is your reputation at stake, your good conscience needs to remain intact. Be smart about what clients you agree to take on and under what circumstances. Any *leader* worth their title will be happy to work openly with an executive coach because they know they will only improve their effectiveness by becoming more self-aware. Do not compromise your integrity as a coach and trusted advisor. Insist on common denominators for a successful engagement.

Client Story: Early on I worked with Cynthia, an executive director of a non-profit. The entire year we worked together, I wondered if she was getting any value from our coaching sessions. When I asked her, she assured me that she was indeed getting value. She had no one else she could share her vulnerability with and counted on me to support her leadership values. I was honored to be that person. The sessions progressed as we solidified her board and built her staff so that she could retire in good conscience passing the baton to a capable leader and board.

She invited me to attend her retirement party. When I entered, she proudly introduced me as her life coach. I was pleasantly surprised at this introduction, but not surprised by her dignified poise. This was a big celebration with many people from the business and the community showing up to honor her with their stories about Cynthia and her impact as a leader. She exemplified transparent leadership. Cynthia set the bar as my ideal client.

When you notice you are working with your ideal client and can hardly believe they chose you to coach them, take notes regarding their qualities. Place these notes in your business plan and document your ideal client profile so you can refer to this profile and the specific qualities you look for in an ideal client. By clarifying your ideal client, you will more easily attract this person. You both will recognize each other in synchronistic moments as I did when I walked into Cynthia's office at the very moment she was considering hiring a coach.

At each quarterly evaluation, assess whether your client is making progress from coaching and revise the primary focus areas. It may be that priorities have changed, with new items added or old items removed. Honor your client's mission and vision and help them clarify both. Keep these statements close at hand for practice. Teach your client to use the law of attraction by committing their mission and vision to memory and stating them out loud, with great emotion twice a day.

Exploring Your Mission and Vision

Stay inspired to live your dream by staying connected with your passion. Pay attention to what lights your fire. Stoke that fire by acting upon that which excites you. When do you feel most alive? What environment is best for you to thrive in? What business leaders do you want to get to know at a deeper level to help them attain their goals? Is there something about their mission that you believe in and can help support? Notice when you light up or when you get excited. Excitement is the emotional clue that you are passionate and on the right path.

You know that you are passionate about being authentic and helping others be happy, fulfilled, and successful in life. When you are helping others discover their passion, you are offering your unique talents and gifts and giving them permission to follow their passion. You inspire others because you are clearly passionate. That passion in you attracts others. You are clearer than most about what is important to you. You can shift the culture with your ability to express your passion. You are a leader and your ability to communicate clearly with passion causes others to listen and question the choices and decisions they make in life. You help others see reality more clearly and take more responsibility for their actions to live a healthier happier life. You can change the world.

Review Your Mission and Vision

Because you are clear about the difference you want to make in the world by helping people follow their passion, you simply need to review your mission before you approach a prospective client.

As you come across obstacles, use your business plan as a place to get inspired and motivated. Review your mission, vision, and values regularly and as things evolve, revise accordingly. You will be reminded of the problem you see in the world and the effect you want to have on it.

Once you realize that you are passionate about making the world a happier place for all, you may want to refine your mission and vision. Your mission is the effect you wish to have on the world. Your mission may be to make people happy at work, and lead from a place of authenticity and service. Your vision is how you see the world in an ideal state of being. Your vision may be a world full of engaged workers, entrepreneurs, and business leaders self-actualizing themselves and their organizations. As a result, everyone is provided the proper environment to achieve their full potential, not just the privileged, but each person in the company.

I see a world of happy people working toward something bigger than themselves inspired to get to work to further a cause. Their cause may be creating a healthier community, a more beautiful world, a more prosperous planet, or more fulfillment in people's lives.

Finding a Need in the Marketplace

Personal Story: When I was working in corporate headquarters of a large technology company and dealing with my own personal struggle of feeling split as a working mother, I noticed other colleagues in the hallway who appeared lost or disillusioned. I recall one day stopping to talk to one fellow colleague asking what he did in our company and how his department fit into the overall picture. I could tell right away he was unhappy at work. Appearing mystified by my questions, he was unable to provide an answer. He had no idea how his department's role fit within the company's mission or vision. He was a lost soul disengaged at work due to poor communication from his leader. He stayed because he had a family and a mortgage.

Years later, reviewing global survey data as a coach, I found that 87% of the working world is disengaged at work. It became obvious that it is not enough that a job pays the mortgage. The company mission, vision and work itself must bring personal fulfillment. Below is an example of a disengaged worker. This is what can happen when you continually ignore your inner wisdom.

Personal Story: I was speaking with a fellow manager over lunch. She ran a call center and was exhausted sharing about a typical week and the number of hours she worked. When I asked her about her passion, she hesitated with a blank stare. Confused, she said, "You know, I used to have a passion, but I have forgotten what that was." This was heartbreaking news to me. I never wanted to be in her position having forgotten my passion. Take note. Never lose sight of your passion!

Now that I have determined my passion, followed my heart, and created a successful business doing what I love, I want to help others experience that personal freedom and follow their heart. It is tragic that so many people are still stuck and likely confused about their passion or have ignored it so long it has shriveled up from lack of care having been forgotten. Too many people are going into work each day miserable. It is an epidemic worthy of investment of time to find a cure.

It is much healthier to know what you are passionate about and do work that feeds that passion. Then each day you will be excited to begin your work. You believe in yourself and the mission you are on. I believe strongly that each of us must take personal responsibility to do what we love and forge our path to success. Many of us need support to be true to ourselves and find a way to be authentic. I thoroughly enjoy supporting leaders in achieving their dreams and becoming more effective and inspirational.

My mission is to see a world of happy people doing what they love. I want everyone at work to experience the sentiments articulated by Khalil Gibran, "Work is love made visible."

Talent Meets Market Need

As I studied where I might take my desire to coach others and match this with the needs of the marketplace for my talents, gifts, and skills, I found by reading global coaching studies that the highest need for coaches was in leadership. I decided since I was already attracting leaders to my coaching business, that I would focus my efforts on CEOs. This way, I could leverage my time, be paid well, and work with fewer clients to maintain my life balance and priority as a mother. I could make a big impact on society by working with leaders at the highest level and count on the ripple effect.

Become an Expert

Notice what area of executive coaching you are drawn to and hone your skills through research, continuing education, and practice. I have developed expertise by helping leaders develop their self-awareness, executive presence, interpersonal skills, and overall emotional intelligence. I am a fan of authentic leadership and servant leadership. My focus is listening for passion and giving my clients permission to do what they want to do and to stay focused on that to become the person and leader they envision in its highest form. Start where you are and go where your passion leads you.

Honor your vision and mission as you build your ideal clientele. Help cure the disengaged worker epidemic. Work with business leaders and entrepreneurs to change the world. Honor your client's mission and vision by drawing it out of them and clarifying both for them. Help your client articulate their mission and vision to maintain a crystal-clear focus.

Chapter 7:

Key 5 – Explore Stakeholder Feedback

*"What is necessary to change a person
is to change his awareness of himself."*
– Abraham Maslow

To further a leader's self-awareness, it is helpful to gather 360-degree feedback. This involves assessing the client as they see themselves and assessing how others surrounding the client view the client as a leader. In this chapter, you will learn how to obtain feedback from stakeholders, and how to prepare, perform, and deliver a 360-degree feedback report to your client.

Preparing for a 360-Degree Feedback Assessment

To begin the 360-degree feedback process, you will start by reviewing the list of stakeholders your client provided in the intake. The list must contain the key stakeholders and others that your client believes can provide useful feedback, by having witnessed your client in interactions over at least six months.

Stakeholders are those that have a stake in the outcome of the coaching candidate's executive coaching. Obtain input from your client's superior to ensure their agreement with the list of stakeholders and modify as needed. Always provide your client with the finalized list so that there are no surprises. You should have approximately twelve stakeholders on the list. Include at least one superior (boss or board member), five peers, and five direct reports, plus external customers where appropriate.

Prepare a generic email for your client and have them edit it or write their own. Ask your client to send each participant or "rater" an email explaining the process. For example:

> *I am focusing on my leadership skills and would appreciate your participation in the 360-degree feedback process by meeting with Donna Karaba from Karaba Consulting on August 8 at two p.m. The interview will last approximately forty-five minutes and your feedback will remain confidential. Your feedback will be aggregated and provided to me in a report highlighting my strengths and areas of development. I will keep you informed as to my progress and appreciate your input.*
>
> *See sample 360 participant letters here:*
> *www.karabaconsulting.com/clientforms*

360-Degree Survey Tools – Qualitative and Quantitative

Having over ten years' experience providing executive feedback, I have evolved my 360-degree feedback approach. First, I ensure that the coaching engagement with the client is open to all stakeholders/raters. Second, I begin the 360-degree feedback process in our initial meeting by gathering a list of raters. Third, I ensure the client's superior agrees with the list of raters and both the client and superior sign off on the final list. Fourth, I engage key stakeholders in the 360-degree process with brief quarterly surveys and feedback. In indirect coaching engagements meet with the primary stakeholders for an hour a month to provide status updates, build rapport, and gain important insight into the company direction to assist in client development.

The 360-degree process is most effective when it is interactive between the stakeholders and the candidate. Review the interview data with the client, help them create an action plan, and then provide an update with high level data from the interviews to the stakeholders including key strengths and one or two areas of development. I like to reiterate client strengths and the development area of focus at the start of the follow up survey process to remind the stakeholders what behaviors they are being asked to observe and support. I see my role as client champion reporting progress as it relates to coaching.

The first round of stakeholder interviews includes survey questions to draw out the coaching candidate's strengths and areas where the client can improve. The follow up interviews are much shorter reiterating the client's strengths and the area of improvement. Ask two simple questions: 1) How would you rate this area of development on a scale of one to five (or whatever scale you wish to use)? and 2) Describe the reason for your rating. Once you gather this feedback, go back to your client and review the action plan to adjust where necessary. Each month you can provide progress updates to key stakeholders in writing and or by phone. You need to manage both the coaching candidate and the client company stakeholder expectations.

Discuss the process with the key stakeholders to understand their needs and set expectations on how you plan to proceed. The framework I have shared is a structure that allows for your own style. As you grow your practice, you may find a best practice that works for you.

Schedule Stakeholder Interviews

Ask your client to have their assistant set up forty-five-minute interviews back-to-back on the hour with all the key stakeholders. Include space for lunch and do not schedule more than six interviews a day (find what works for you). Perform these in person if possible. Videoconference (via Zoom or Skype) is an option for remote interviews, those that are unable to meet in person. Provide two or three days to complete the interviews.

The assistant will send you the schedule for the interviews with meeting room times and locations. This may be on-site if there is a confidential meeting room space, or reserve a boardroom at a nearby hotel and share the address with the candidate's assistant who is lining up interviews.

Perform Interviews with Stakeholders

Prepare a list of questions after studying the 360-degree process doing some research into the various tools available.

You can see the list of questions I use here: www.karabaconsulting.com/clientforms

Meet with each stakeholder in the designated meeting room. Thank the participant for agreeing to provide helpful feedback. Explain that your conversation is confidential, and information will be aggregated so that the client will not know who said what. Ask for permission to record the interview so you do not rely on heavy note taking and can instead remain more present. If the interviewee shows any concern, such as a new direct report, do not record the interview and take notes as needed in writing or on the computer (whichever works for you). Explain to those that are okay with being recorded that this is meant only to supplement your notes and will be erased once your report is completed. I typically have no problem with people feeling uncomfortable being recorded. Just be sensitive if someone appears uncomfortable. Explain the 360-degree assessment process briefly and then begin asking your open-ended questions to engage the interviewee in dialogue.

Gather and Analyze 360-Degree Feedback Data

Type up notes from your interviews listening to recorded interviews. Code data by person for each question to ensure you have a representative sample of data rather than weighted to only a few participants' feedback. Read through the data and gather essential points made that will benefit your client's growth. Type up your feedback report and focus on strengths. Find the primary area for development. If there is more than one area, be careful not to overwhelm the client with more than two areas of development. Be compassionate and empathetic to your client's feelings as you share the feedback (more on this in chapter eight). It is helpful to present the feedback sharing client strengths, the one or two areas of development and end by emphasizing their strengths. Everyone has areas to develop, and most people do not acknowledge their own strengths. This is a perfect opportunity for your client to receive positive feedback and helpful insights to be most effective in their leadership role.

Prepare 360-Degree Assessment Feedback Report

Use the 360-degree feedback report template found here: www. karabaconsulting.com/clientforms or feel free to create your own 360 feedback report design. List your client strengths and one or two areas of development. Summarize in a confidential report for the client. Work with your client to prepare an executive summary of the report to share with key stakeholders along with an action plan. Ensure your client provides this report to all stakeholders, or in some cases you may wish to provide the executive summary in your follow up meetings with stakeholders. This process will engage stakeholder support.

Ensure your coaching candidate has met with their boss to review the executive summary report. This report should be high level as there is no need for details to engage stakeholder support.

Evaluate progress quarterly with stakeholders using a brief survey (see www.karabaconsulting.com/clientforms) to determine level of client progress and follow up by the client. Note your client progress.

Focus on strengths. Here are some actual strengths from client feedback reports:

- Strong Leader – leads by example
- Knowledgeable – understands a variety of areas in the industry
- Experienced – has vast experience in the industry, moves people to the right places
- Accessible – involved, available, really helpful
- Capable – makes decisions based on facts, very smart
- Adaptable – always willing to help and works to adapt to personalities, situations, and people
- Dedicated – puts in long days and gets good results
- Collaborative – holds leadership staff meetings every other week, and other important team meetings weekly, open to ideas
- Helpful – discusses plans and makes suggestions
- Direct – straight to the point, stops attitudes amongst team members, promotes camaraderie, stays level-headed, stands their ground
- Value Driven – honest, wants to do what is right
- Fair – treats people with respect, does not show favoritism
- Supportive – allows managers to make decisions and supports them, respected by others, if someone has a better idea, willing to listen and go with it, supports staff decisions, and backs them with internal and external customers

- Teacher – takes time to explain things, says things like, "I like your ability to ask questions," encouraging, shows no arrogance with knowledge, shares freely
- Team Player – gets managers involved even when it does not seem necessary, willing to reach out for help when needed
- Organized – manages day well, involved in internal and external projects

Here are some areas to improve effectiveness gathered from actual client feedback reports:

- Communicate: Communicate privately when frustrated with individuals. Pause and breathe to diffuse issues before they escalate.
- Value Differences: Be patient with individuals who differ in style, look for the value each team member brings.
- Listen: Acknowledge ideas and input from others. Demonstrate listening by summarizing what you have heard using their words.
- Collaborate: Show your openness to work with others. Express your willingness to try new ideas and empower staff to implement their ideas. Brainstorm to incorporate input from others. Have an open agenda to allow room for teamwork and unexpected outcomes.
- Respond: Take responsibility and take appropriate action when leaders question quality of work. Address issues with team and coach members to deliver high-quality deliverables and bring in outside expertise when necessary. Pay attention to different audiences' needs and how they require different levels of information.
- Strategic Planning: Frame issues properly when presenting to others. Approach people in advance and allow them to plan their resources. Continually consider how to use contacts

strategically. Take the perspective of a leader of the organization and treat business objectives as a higher priority than departmental objectives. Articulate high level cohesive strategic statements.

Deliver 360-Degree Feedback Report

You will work with a wide spectrum of leaders and abilities. 360-degree feedback is easy to deliver to a rising star, an admired leader, or an ideal client. Other times, 360-degree feedback is not easy to deliver. In either case, I focus on the client's strengths because too often a client does not recognize their strengths. Leadership is often a thankless job, and lonely. Granted, there are perks to being in a leadership role such as status, compensation, and prestige, yet on the other hand, when things go wrong, who takes the blame? The leader.

Deliver feedback to your client with compassion, kindness, and respect. Consider how you would want your own 360-degree feedback delivered. Your clients will appreciate the emphasis on their strengths and most will be open to areas of development. You can be tough by getting straight to the point even when that is uncomfortable. Just be kind. Remember to always start and end on a positive note.

Finally, allow your client some time to digest the results of the 360-degree assessment on their own and develop an action plan. You can provide suggestions for the action plan and work together to put this in place. Depending on the type of 360-degree feedback process you agreed to with the key stakeholders, ensure the client shares the action plan with all the stakeholders including you.

Client Story: Brian was in the position of leader by default. He was not happy, clearly stressed by an underperforming business unit. He acted out through sarcasm with staff. As we explored his talents and interests, he found a more suitable position in another business unit that utilized his strengths maintaining an influen-

tial position in the company. He is much happier and is provid-
ing more value to the organization. A win-win.

As a coach you have greater insight at times for your client's best interest than they do themselves and sometimes they need validation and permission to find a better fit. It is your job to help your client be successful and happy. If your client is not called to be in the position they have landed in, it is best for everyone if they evaluate their strengths, talents, and skills in relation to their passion and purpose and pursue avenues where they can be of greater help to the organization.

As you engage new clients you will be continually challenged to learn how to help people develop in specific areas. I cannot tell you how many books I have read on a client's behalf to teach a new skill. For example, I am reading seven books right now for different clients and different reasons. Some are resources I have read in the past for a different client, some are new topics based on client needs. See my online library as reference. Very often I send clients books as homework assignments to help teach them what they need to know for their specific professional development issue. Each client is in a different role and stage of life. The variety of clients and their unique personalities make the work both fascinating and challenging. Gaining stakeholder feedback will reveal blind spots for your client and provide insight into the organizational culture and variety of perspectives.

You can find my favorite reference books here:
www.karabaconsulting.com/library

As you begin a new client relationship, include the 360 degree assessment process. Done well, you and your client can gain excellent feedback that will fuel the growth of your client. You can use both qualitative, in-person interviews, and quantitative, on-line surveys, to gain necessary perspectives on your client's effectiveness as a leader.

Find a format that suits the needs of your client situation. When I have the free reign to assess my client, I use every assessment I am qualified to use, for example my own qualitative process utilizing the 360-degree feedback questions, and quantitative surveys like MBTI, Executive Dimensions, Benchmarks for Managers and ESCI. My goal is to build my client's self-awareness to allow for more personal and professional growth.

Chapter 8:

Key 6 – Nurture Highest Self

"Be the one who nurtures and builds. Be the one who has an understanding and a forgiving heart one who looks for the best in people. Leave people better than you found them."
– Marvin J. Ashton

A coach nurtures the seed within, one's highest self. You, as an executive coach, will address the very important, ineffable, inner world of your clients. I choose to use different words to describe this internal seed. You will see me using higher self, passion, soul, spirit, essence, and true self. If there is a name you prefer, please substitute it wherever you like.

When I performed a job I was not passionate about, I felt as if I had to check my soul at the door as I swiped my key card to enter the building. Only my mind and body were welcome. I could pick my spirit up on my way out. My soul's only acknowledgment came when I went to yoga. Yoga became my most compelling reason for coming to work toward the end of my last corporate job because yoga allowed me to honor my highest self and tolerate the toxic political environment.

We each can be most effective when our whole selves are welcome and honored at work. If we find our whole self not acknowledged at work, we are most definitely in the wrong place and need to search for the right environment.

Just as a plant needs the proper environment to grow and blossom, so does your higher self. With 87% of employees disengaged at work this means that *most* people are not eager to wake up each morning to get to work. How sad is that?! Most people waste precious moments in life because they do not realize they have a choice.

Your job as an executive coach following the Authentic Leadership Business Model™ is to treat that delicate seed with loving care! Your goal is to provide an optimal environment in which that seed can grow and develop to its full potential.

Imagine you are an angel with a master key, unlocking (self-created) prison doors, releasing spirits to do great work in the world. That image keeps me inspired to do this work. Most of your clients are stuck inside their imaginary prisons – prisons they are unaware that they have built. Your role is to release their passion and get them on track with their authentic purpose. Your client must see how their leadership can authentically serve others.

How do you nurture that seed? How do you create a safe environment where that seed can blossom? How do you remove the weeds?

It is helpful to remember that you are working with precious souls. You have built a strong foundation in your own life, developing the awareness to be fully present and loving with the souls you are fortunate to work with. You have an innate ability to draw out another person's passion. You also have an educated practice developing your presence to be a loving witness of that passion and allow their higher self to have a voice. When that voice has safe space, it gets louder and louder. At first, you may be the only one to hear that voice, and that is how you can help your client nurture the seed within, by giving their spirit's voice a chance to be heard out loud. You can think of yourself as a midwife, helping birth a soul by drawing out passion and helping your client take action. Each action is like water or sunshine nurturing the seed within. You are teaching your client how to provide an ideal environment for that seed to blossom to its full potential. Once your client can hear that voice within loud and clear, decisive actions become clear and help move your client forward.

When I deliver feedback, I remember how delicate the soul is. My intention is to nurture the higher self and acknowledge my client's strengths. I explain to my client that their strengths support their authentic leadership capabilities and style.

Some feedback can be jarring, and thus feedback needs to be shared with care. By focusing on only one or two areas of development you and your client's work will have the most impact. Change is not easy. Self-awareness is what we are truly going for, because often the areas that are perceived as needing development are areas that the client is not aware of. In other words, the client has blind spots and as soon as light is shed on these areas, the client has choice in the matter and can do something about it. That area was merely off the radar screen entirely.

By providing 360-degree assessments, you can more effectively aid your clients in developing their authentic leadership styles, thus increasing their effectiveness at work. Your clients' exceptional results will lead to more business for them which is what you had intended as a by-product of executive coaching. As your clients build stronger relationships in their lives, you will see their business grow. Remember to treat their highest self with tenderness and care. By doing so, you will allow a safe space for their potential to blossom.

Chapter 9:

Key 7 – Teach Gaps in Leadership

"Leaders who listen are able to create
trustworthy relationships that are
transparent and breed loyalty.
You know the leaders who have their
employees' best interests at heart
because they truly listen to them."
– Glenn Llopis

Now that you have delivered the 360-degree feedback report, it is time to explore the gaps between where your client is and where your client wants to be. As a coach, you will teach your client specific leadership skills incorporating the client stakeholders' objectives, candidate objectives, and 360-degree feedback. With new insights, the client can decide how best to practice their strengths and new skills to become more effective.

Executive Coaching Session Format for 360-Degree Feedback Action Plan

Client Story: After completing Gretchen's 360 interviews, I found that the main area of development was "listening" and the second area was "collaboration." I explained to Gretchen that everyone in the 360 has a different set of needs and expectations and therefore a different lens in which they view her. Gretchen has her own perspective of herself as a leader. My job is to expose the multiple realities Gretchen works in as each individual perspective is its own reality. This 360 information will help her see herself through these various lenses, thus increasing her self-awareness and her ability to detect the unique needs of others. Navigating in the same environment aided by new insights, Gretchen will have more options to choose her response.

As I described her strengths, Gretchen was very touched. She was pleased to hear what people appreciated and noticed in her leadership capabilities. As I shared areas of development, Gretchen was most surprised that listening was her primary area of development. She perceived herself to be a very good listener and valued this quality in others. Yet, the feedback was clear that people perceived her as being so focused on her own agenda for meetings, that she did not leave an opening to hear input from others. Others perceived her as not being open to listening and were left with the impression that she did not care about their input or ideas.

Noticing the wide gap in Gretchen's self-perception as a listener, I needed to help her raise her self-awareness to be able to witness and manage the impact she had on others. Even though she believed she was listening and may have been listening more than people realized, Gretchen was not demonstrating her openness to others. We had work to do. We needed to increase her ability to listen and demonstrate that she was hearing what others were saying to actively manage perceptions.

First, we discussed several basic levels of listening that I learned as a coach.

Level 1: What does it mean to me? I hear the words being said and I am focused on what it means to me. I am looking inside myself as I listen. I hear what you are saying and internalize the impact on me.

Level 2: What does it mean to you? I hear what you are saying, and I am trying to understand what it means to you.

Level 3: I hear what you are saying word for word and I am not distracted by my own thoughts. I notice the energy being expressed and the energy in the environment and what you may or may not be saying. I notice the vocal speed and pitch, body language, facial expressions, movements, emotions, and tears. I also may notice my own intuition, body emotions, or pain and can reflect this back to you as wisdom and insight into your life. (Techniques based on Whitworth, Kimsey-House, and Sandall's research in 1998.)

I also shared some techniques that Gretchen could practice with each opportunity to listen. First, I told her to be fully present as she listens. I taught her how to meditate and tame the mind to calm the constant flow of thoughts. Discursive or rambling thoughts can get in the way of listening if you are not aware of those thoughts. I taught her to focus her attention on the person speaking. Inhale deeply and exhale deeply before responding. I suggested she pause and ask herself, "Is what I am about to say helpful in this situation?" Listening at an advanced level may bring up sensations in the body or an image in the mind that has to do with what is happening with the other person. I suggested she pay attention to her thoughts and feelings, and the intuitive hits which may come up as a flashing image in the mind, or a feeling in the body. "If the image or feeling is not normal for you," I explained, "it may be what the other person is thinking or feeling. You can check in with that person if you feel it might be helpful."

I shared my own experiences developing my listening skills after deepening my meditation practice. I became more self-aware and present with my clients, thus I paid attention more fully. I was able to stay present and not be distracted by my own thoughts. I was able to notice intuitive hits listening by phone to clients. Once, I felt a constriction in my throat, and shared this odd feeling with my client. The phone went silent. She then explained through tears as she released pent up emotion recalling how she felt as a child having no voice in her family. With another client, I saw turtles as she was speaking to me in a quiet voice over the phone. I shared the unusual image in my mind to see if it had any meaning to her. Surprised by this, my client said that she was literally surrounded by a collection of turtles she had in her home.

Listening is a very useful skill to hone as a leader. The more you practice it, the more information you can pick up in a conversation through tone of voice or energy exchange and receive as intuitive wisdom, physical sensations, or mental images.

The ability to listen is the most common area requiring development in leadership feedback. The cause may be that the client has not developed their listening ability, or has not demonstrated their ability to listen, or both. The focus must be on what the person is saying, what it means to them, and what else they are communicating through voice, energy, and body language. Gretchen needed to develop self-awareness by clearing the mind of mental chatter, suspend judgment, and pay more attention to the impact her behavior was having on the other person speaking. She was not using dialogue to demonstrate she was hearing what the other person was saying. I shared that it is possible that people's perception of her was wrong only because she did not share verbally what she heard them say. It is possible she merely needed to work on changing their perception by changing the way in which she communicated her ability to listen.

I provided Gretchen a book solely focused on the topic of listening. This way she could dig deeper into the intricacies of listening understanding various contexts. Together we came up with several techniques to help her demonstrate listening. At Gretchen's follow-up 360, her stakeholders reported that she made dramatic improvements in her ability to listen.

See my recommended book list here:
www.karabaconsulting.com/library

Student Story: Based on some of my experiences at Naropa, I decided to take my coaching students, those that made it all the way through the program, to a local state park to celebrate the completion of the leadership coaching program. I wanted to give them an experience in nature to practice listening and reflection. I set up a sacred threshold and explained the ritual. I began by explaining that we were going to walk in nature in complete silence. As each student crossed the threshold they were to walk mindfully through the woods following me on a walking meditation listening to the sounds of nature. Each would then find a spot to sit and reflect on their experience. They could draw or write about something in nature or write about their silent walk. After about 30 minutes of reflection, I guided our group back out and across the threshold. My intention was to teach them to listen in a mindful way. I wanted them to not only listen to sounds of nature, but to take in the full experience as the observer. I also wanted to give them time to listen internally and write or draw whether their experience they were reflecting upon was internal or external.

One student, Brenda, shared that she had never been out in nature her entire life. She was twenty years old. She was profoundly impacted by this nature experience and promised herself she would spend more time reflecting in nature. Another student, Emily, had an awakening that medicine was not her ideal field of study. She had pursued it to provide for her parents in old age. Instead she decided to follow her passion to become an educator. As Emily shared this epiphany she was tearing up and I had a flashback as though I was speaking to my younger self and wondered where she would be in twenty five years. I felt honored to witness these students be profoundly impacted by the program.

Examining the gaps and coaching your clients from where they are now to where they want to be, empowers them to make meaningful change. Take a look at the leadership and life wheels you completed with your client and update the primary focus areas regularly to ensure you are helping your client close the gap between where they are now and where they want to be as a leader and in life.

Chapter 10:

Key 8 – Investigate ROI for Sustainability

"When you love someone, the best thing you can offer is your presence. How can you love if you are not there?"
– Thich Nhat Hanh

The key to becoming a successful coach is to be fully present with your clients. Be loving, honest, and kind. You develop solid relationships by caring about your clients' success and happiness. These business relationships will last years – some your entire career. People trust you when you genuinely care about them. Your natural ability with people is a quality that will enable you to create friends, champions who will stand behind you, and long-term business relationships.

You have partnered with your client to understand their business goals and thus have operated with clarity. You clarified up front what was at stake for a successful outcome. You asked the right questions meeting with key stakeholders before you began the coaching assignment to understand your client's business goals. Now you can review your results with your key stakeholders, for example:

1. You stated that the reason you hired me to coach this candidate was to develop this leader to succeed senior executives and maintain relationships with internal and external customers who are key stakeholders in a $200M project. What growth have you seen in the candidate toward this goal?

2. We decided that we would know that this coaching engagement was successful if the candidate demonstrated strategic thinking and inspired his team with a clear vision. On a scale of zero to ten, how much progress have you seen the client make toward this goal?

3. Let's review the actual bottom line result of coaching this leader. What was saved in recruiting and replacement costs? How much was saved by maintaining key relationships? What is the value to the company of completing this $200M project?

4. What growth have you seen in the client?

This kind of analysis is not essential. It may help you realize the success of the work being done. My clients have never requested an ROI evaluation, but I believe it may save you agony over pricing and self-doubt as to the value your client receives. You may not need to prove your value to your clients, because it is obvious to them. You may only need to prove your value to yourself as you build your confidence. If you can quantify the total value of the worth of the assignment – what it would cost the company to lose this employee at this time, or what the client company will gain by developing the executive – the information will help you justify your fee to yourself. This work is priceless. Believe in yourself!

Having priced your services at the range you are comfortable working, determine now how much value you brought the company by solving this problem. Review the estimated ROI to the actual ROI to understand how much the company gained realizing the coaching objectives. Price your services according to the value you bring.

Systems for Success

Develop a system to manage and evaluate your client stakeholder goals for the coaching engagement. Set up monthly check-in meetings with your key stakeholders. Review progress of the client coaching engagement(s) and determine any new expectations that might have come up between check-ins. If the scope of work changes, you may need to revise your agreement, or if agreed upon, invoice for additional consulting. Provide high level updates based on terms of the coaching engagement.

Quarterly, evaluate the objectives and gain feedback based on client developmental goals. Ask open-ended questions to stakeholders to obtain specific feedback regarding behavioral shifts with the coaching candidate. Evaluate changes using a simple number scale. Document this quarterly feedback as part of the 360-degree feedback process. Provide high-level progress to key stakeholders.

Gain any testimonials that naturally come out of conversations. Request the use of the testimonial with your client's full name, title, and company logo in your marketing materials. (You may wish to include this in your retainer agreement verbiage and cover this up front.) You need champions who obtained great value from your work to support your business development efforts.

How Do I Stay on Track with My Business Plan?

Review your business plan quarterly. Hire or befriend a mentor coach who can help you move through fear. Consider joining a local coaching chapter through the International Coach Federation.

Develop discipline in your business. Schedule an ideal time of day to work on marketing and sales. Determine days of the week or once a month where you will keep track of your financials, including invoicing, bill paying, bookkeeping, and taxes. Find ways to stay motivated and focused by setting up a workout schedule. Do what you enjoy helping to clear your mind and manage stress. Swim, bike, dance, walk, or run. Find a workout buddy or join active groups to support your healthy habits.

Include a variety of self-care habits to maintain optimal health and balance of mind, body, and spirit practicing meditation, yoga, and affirmations. Join a meditation community to practice with (in Buddhist terms, "Sangha") for group support to ensure you acknowledge your spirit and keep meditating. I find that groups are not only friendly and engaging, they also provide a wonderful reminder to keep up your personal practice. For your daily practice, you can start by reading an inspirational book, or download a guided meditation app to your phone to make your sitting practice easier. Locate a space amenable to silence and calm or create one and set a timer to develop a daily habit. It only takes 21 days of consistent practice to develop a new habit. Mark your calendar and just do it. You will be grateful you persevered and developed this powerful habit.

Take care of yourself by balancing mind, body and spirit – this balance is crucial to the success of your business. Feel good physically and emotionally to create sustainability in your business. Research the return on investment that your client receives due to your coaching. Price your services accordingly ensuring you are well compensated for the value you provide. Valuable client engagements and disciplined self-care will lead to a thriving business.

Chapter 11:

Key 9 – Cultivate New Business

"Don't judge each day by the harvest you reap but by the seeds that you plant."
– Robert Louis Stevenson

Business Development

Now that you have identified your ideal client and know what you can offer them, research their business to understand their mission, vision, and values and the marketplace where they fit. Reach out to them, providing your elevator pitch, and uncover their current leadership challenges and goals. Your objective is to understand what they desire, so that you can determine how best to help them achieve their goals. Let them know you understand their problem by repeating the problem you heard using their words and explain briefly how you can help them achieve their specific goals. Set up an in-person meeting. Speak to their problem and explain how you can help them reach their objectives. Listen and use their words as you restate their goals. Be confident and sincere about your ability to help them.

If a client is eager for your help, create a proposal to provide executive coaching for one year and bring the proposal with you to your meeting. Greet your client with confidence and explore their needs and listen actively. Clearly communicate their problem, their goal, and how you can help them get from here to there. Walk your ideal client through your proposal, assuming they are ready to work with you. Hand your prospective client your pen to sign your agreement. If your client signs the agreement, schedule your appointments to create space for your client and allow them to create space to work with you. Congratulations! You have closed an ideal client.

That is the ideal scenario I have used to build my business. Think of it as an experiment and with each experiment, learn something new and refine your process. Track your statistics of calls, contacts, meetings, and clients to determine your close rate.

Developing Your Proposal

Be confident as you approach businesses. Once you understand the needs of the client organization by speaking to the key stakeholder(s), you can develop your proposal and submit it to the person responsible for engaging your services. This can be as simple as a one-page retainer agreement outlining the services you will provide. Include 1:1 executive coaching, meeting in person or by phone twice a month or more, a 360-degree feedback assessment, and the term of the agreement: annual retainer. (Note: Do not quote less than six months even if you are just trying to get a foot in the door.) Once the client agrees to your proposal by providing their signature, and you receive your first payment in advance, you have a client. You are ready to schedule your first coaching appointment. If you do not wish to be so formal with an agreement, you can send a brief proposal in an email and obtain confirmation from your client with a written reply.

Client Story: As I was preparing one of my first proposals to a prospective CEO client, Mark, I also prepared a manual to clearly share my process. I had learned from a previous CEO meeting that this question might come up and I wanted to have an articulate answer. I felt very confident that Mark, a new prospect was ready to engage my services based on our phone conversations. I prepared both my proposal and executive coaching manual so that I could walk him through the process, share example coaching tools, and close the business with a signed agreement.

I arrived as planned, thirty minutes prior to our appointment. I sat in the parking lot and meditated to calm my nerves. I then rehearsed in my mind the flow of the meeting all the way to Mark signing my executive coaching agreement. The meeting went exactly as planned. He allowed me to direct the flow. He explained how his business got started and how his leadership team was set up. He wanted me to understand his business. He appeared genuinely interested in my materials, underlining steps in the process and key content as he was reading. I handed him my pen and proceeded to close the business as he signed the agreement.

This was my first CEO client engagement. As I drove out of the parking lot, I played back mentally how smoothly the meeting went. It was time to celebrate my success. I stopped and purchased a favorite tea, a treat to myself to commemorate the moment. I sat there sipping my tea, savoring the splendid feeling of excitement of having a new ideal client to work with and the sense of accomplishment from proper preparation. It is very important to celebrate your wins! Success breeds success. Mark became a long-term client and a champion of mine.

Create a Marketing Funnel

As a business owner, you will need to create a marketing funnel, or a continual flow of leads that can become prospects and eventually clients. I used cold calling CEOs and executives as my initial marketing funnel to generate prospects and clients. If cold calling is not for you, you can choose another route to secure business with your ideal clients. Refer to your business plan. You have your target defined. What are the criteria you developed that describes in detail your ideal client? Using your criterion, determine where your ideal client hangs out and find a way to reach your ideal client.

Speaking and Writing

Are you able to stand up in front of a crowd and speak about your passions? Are you able to sit and write about your passions? These are two great ways to attract people who need what you have to offer.

Every time I speak in front of an audience, I have attracted clients. I know from my experience, that at least one person will connect with your message and want to talk with you afterward. You must have a marketing funnel in place. At a minimum, you want to obtain their email address and offer them a product or service that meets their needs right now. You can create a client on the spot or develop that prospect into a client with a lead magnet. You may want to host an event where you will speak inviting people you know including your clients.

If you prefer writing, you can submit articles to online or print magazines and again have the funnel available to convert readers to clients. Or, you can do what I am doing and write a book about your business. Even if you have just begun, write, speak, get out into the world, and let people know you exist and are ready and able to help them. Remember, people care more about how much you care than how much you know. This wisdom continues to ring true.

Perhaps you will create leads by speaking at local golf clubs, Rotary meetings, or chambers of commerce. Once you have your ideal hook that generates leads you may want to advertise by running ads. You can also message your targeted group on social media platforms such as Linked In, Facebook, or Instagram. You can refine the online community target market profile by matching it to your ideal client profile. You may enjoy writing articles in a business periodical in print or online, write a blog, host a podcast, or be a guest on podcasts speaking about an area of expertise that will draw your ideal clientele to your website. On your website you have a landing page where you offer a free product in exchange for an email address to help you build your community and provide a way for people to contact you.

When I first started doing my own concerted business development with a list of local business owners and executives' names and phone numbers in my local area, I thought it was pure luck that I landed my first client or two. When I closed my third client, I was confident it was more than luck. I was able to create new business for myself by sharing my philosophy of leadership and desire to coach executives.

I befriended a local executive coach who became a mentor. He helped me tremendously over the years as I hit obstacles in developing my business.

Years after I started my business, I moved to another state and once again focused on business development. I attended a workshop on authenticity at a nearby retreat center and asked the workshop leader and author how much time he spends on business development. I thought he might say ten percent of the time, considering he was an accomplished author and workshop leader. I was not expecting to hear the answer he gave me. He spends 50 percent of his time marketing himself! I was stunned.

I considered how much time I was spending on my own business development and was certainly not spending half of my work hours marketing my services. With my current system of making calls about three months a year, I had somehow managed to run a profitable business without a published book or fifty percent of my time devoted to business development. Still it caused me to pause and wonder, "How *do* you sustain a consulting business?"

Realizing the ebb and flow of business, I recommend doing business development fifty percent of the time and at an absolute minimum, twenty-five percent. To keep your business off the ground and soaring, you need a continual flow of clients coming on board which means you need a continual flow of leads and prospects. If you have three solid CEO long-term relationships you may be able to get away with the minimum as these may, if you are very fortunate, provide you a lifetime of work. If you have three to five major client companies, you are likely doing very well as a sole proprietor.

When you open your business, you will devote 100 percent of your effort on business development. As you obtain your foundation of clients, you will adjust your business development effort. Remember that the economy fluctuates and impacts various industries, so it is a good idea to have many baskets with many eggs in each basket, meaning many different clients in different industries and many clients within each client company. Losing a major client in a small portfolio of client companies can devastate your business and may put you out of business. You want to avoid this by continuously building your client base.

My Business Development Story: I started targeting CEOs in 2006 and by the end of the year, I had made 1,000 calls, made ten executive appointments, and closed four clients from four different companies: a CEO, and three VPs. I had exceeded my personal stretch goal of $100K and booked that by the end of *the year. I was feeling quite fortunate to be doing the work I was doing, devoting as much time as I wanted with my children and husband, able to work around their schedules.*

In 2008, the economy took a big turn, and this resulted in business declines with my major client. In 2010, when my client asked me to cut back on the time I was devoting to his business, I realized that I had put too many eggs in one basket. I had several clients at his business that I was working with and not enough other baskets or eggs. To cut back with this client company, I needed to replace the income with at least another major client.

I hustled to develop a new list of local businesses by starting up my cold calling campaign. I had allowed my business development effort to remain on hold too long. Most businesses do not allow their sales force to shut down for months at a time. With renewed persistent effort, I was able to land two major clients and one small client. That done, I was able to remain in business. That was close!

It is challenging to do business development work while you are working as an executive coach because that is the time you enjoy most in your business doing what you love to do. When you are working with several clients at the same time, especially if they are requiring in-person visits, it seems like more than enough to be the coach, travel agent, and bookkeeper. Each role is time consuming and necessary. Therefore, it is easy to justify dropping the business development effort. Don't!

Create a business development system that keeps you continually qualifying leads and presenting proposals to prospects. I noticed that when I did my business development, I rarely got very far through my alphabetical company lead binder. By the time I called companies beginning with the letter C, it was time to follow up with company letter A. Hence none of my client companies started with the letter H or higher on the alphabet.

There are better ways to automate your prospect list than my manual binder system. Find a way to continuously communicate with your prospects so that you remain in their sight when the need for your services arises.

You have no guarantee of ongoing business with any of your clients. Always keep a full pipeline. In other words, you need enough prospects that are receiving proposals from you continuously to enable you to close new business. I know how tough it is to feel as though you always have your foot on the gas pedal. It can be exhausting to drive hard consistently. It is very tempting and natural to want to take a break when you close new business and start working with a new client. You may not need or want any more business right now. Do not rest long. If you plan and execute your plan consistently, you will not have to switch into high gear and burn out. You will need new business soon enough, so keep reaching out.

Once you have started with your new client, get back to business development. You must be sending proposals to qualified prospects continually if you want to stay independent and in business long term. Your current clients may not last forever. You may be fortunate to have a client or two that want your coaching continuously, but do not count on that. Continually provide value to each client and keep building your base.

If you have accomplished the goals you set out to accomplish with your client and no new goals have been established, check in with your client whether they wish to continue meeting. If your client has received the value they were looking for from you, it may be time to close out the engagement. Document client feedback, ask for referrals, and locate new clients. If your client wishes to continue, you may choose to increase your retainer fee annually.

When you are looking for work, leave no stone unturned. Get to work and look under every rock.

You cannot expect to grow a business without any effort, but do you need to spend half your time developing new business? It depends on where you are in your business. When you begin your business, you need to devote 100 percent of your time developing the business. Once you have your first set of clients and at least a year of business, a good rule of thumb is to spend fifty percent of your time marketing your services. Track your own progress as you build your business and monitor your increasing close rate as you gain experience. Set goals accordingly.

Getting into the Right Mindset to Develop New Business

You need to know yourself and what you find enjoyable when it comes to business development. Do you enjoy talking to people, writing about your field of expertise, or speaking about a particular topic? You may want to try various ways to build your business and then find one that feels good. You must be feeling optimistic and enthusiastic to attract clients. Your emotional state and mental state are key components to growing a business and making new connections. Stay focused on your passion and what lights your fire.

Start your day with a morning meditation and words that inspire you. I have many meditation books on my bookshelf to choose from and often I will read a passage to connect with my higher self – my soul. I give myself a little "soul" food for thought and space to focus the mind and observe my thoughts. By starting out each day this way, you clean the slate of mental chatter and allow your mind to become calm. When your mind is fresh, it will be more creative and useful to you.

The fear stopping you is this, "Am I qualified enough to help CEOs of large businesses or their executive staff?"

I had this same fear as I started my business. Yet, my interest and desire to help people in the business world and improve the quality of leadership doing meaningful work I love was stronger than my fear. I knew I could help others become more self-aware, more authentic, whole, and truer to themselves since I was able to do this in my own life. Having moved through that fear of being qualified and simply starting the work, I was able to help leaders. I was not only impacting their life, I was indirectly impacting the lives of their staff, their family and the rest of the company as well.

There are great leaders in the world, and I am happy I have met them and worked with them enough to see them in action. The problem is that there is a huge deficit of great leaders. This is evident in workforce surveys and employee retention rates. The number one reason people quit their job is due to their relationship with their supervisor.

Workers often feel stuck and unable to see that they have options. With the worker disengagement epidemic, executive coaches can help cure this critical issue by helping leaders grow in their leadership roles providing room for the growth of their co-workers. As an executive coach, I work to help cure this epidemic by helping leaders be their best. These positive interpersonal behavioral shifts in leaders expand the opportunities for thousands of workers. As leaders become more coach-like, they provide an ideal environment for staff.

The Golden Ticket

My naive belief when I became a coach was that everyone would want me to coach them and start calling me to do so. I did not magically turn into fly paper when I became a coach. Quickly I found out that coaching is like any other business, you need to market your product, you, and the services you provide. You need to find leads, qualify those leads, present a proposed solution, and close new business to create clients.

Announcing that you are starting a coaching business is not enough to build a sustainable business. When I made my announcement to my previous colleagues that I was opening a business to coach people, I received one reply which technically started my business. At only $75 per session it was not a model that would come close to replacing a hefty corporate salary and excellent benefits. I needed to charge more and work with more clients.

I needed leads. Because I was once again a poor college student, I did not have money to do paid advertising, or purchase a mailing list, so I went back to what I knew and created a database of leads by going to the library and using my library card. I found company data in the Dunn and Bradstreet database searching the Cincinnati area which was within 45 miles of where we lived at the time. I created a script and purchased a long-distance calling card. I began calling on local CEOs and lined up appointments.

Cold calling may or may not be your first choice. It has worked for me as a low-cost way of advertising. It is a slow process depending how much time and effort you put in, but it does yield consistent results. You may choose to write articles, press releases, books, or start talking to strangers like I did. Whatever way suits you, you will need to let a lot of people know you exist and the specific problems you can solve for them.

When I am wearing my sales hat, I do my best when I imagine I am handing out golden tickets. Remember Charlie's face when he unwraps Willy Wonka's chocolate bar to reveal the golden ticket? My wish is that every person I offer my services to realizes that they just received a golden ticket to my life transformation factory! I am offering my prospects the opportunity to experience that same feeling of joy Charlie felt when he realized he was the lucky one who won the opportunity of a lifetime. He was about to meet the person who would open doors for him allowing Charlie to have his dream come true!

All my prospect needs to do is open the wrapper to reveal their golden ticket. With each contact, I am handing out a golden ticket, a chance for someone to visit my life transformation factory and literally transform their life becoming the person they have dreamed of becoming.

You have that golden ticket, now what are you going to do? You also have a supply of golden tickets to share, who are you going to share them with? Who wants to experience a life of their dreams!

When you get down and full of doubt, remember you have golden tickets to share with other human beings dying to be free, happy, and fulfilled.

Student Story: As I was relaying my Golden Ticket story with a recent student Stefan, he was thrilled with this idea of handing out golden tickets. He was in a funk after losing a large account renewal contract he was expecting. In his quest for more business, he did not want to come across as pushy to his contacts. He is a creative guy with a lot of talent and drive to be a leader in his niche. I just had to remind him how lucky people are to benefit from his talent, skills, experience, and drive. He was excited to reach out to old and new contacts in this new frame of mind that he had a golden ticket for the lucky winner. His energy and enthusiasm for seeking new business was renewed.

When I first started my business, I did not leverage the power of the internet other than to create a website and newsletter. I knew that speaking, writing, and advertising were all very popular tried and true ways to market a business. I tried a variety of approaches, including joining local chambers of commerce, Rotary International, the International Coach Federation, talking to local business press, attending networking events, teaching a continuing education class series, and joining a board. I thought about how I might meet my ideal clients.

I decided that CEOs would be a good target even though it was unlikely I would run into CEOs. I decided to simply call them on the telephone. I visited my local university library and met with a reference librarian who gave me access to research databases and taught me how to search for the information I needed. I used the Dunn and Bradstreet million-dollar database and found how easy it was to obtain the company name, address, and phone of local businesses of a certain size and a certain distance from where I lived. I narrowed the list to thirty companies. I created a script, an elevator pitch along with potential objections and answers.

I knew this cold calling method worked from a business that I started with my husband. He taught me how to cold call leads from the company database and, within six months of trial and error cold calls, I landed a large client for $300K in revenue with guaranteed product purchases throughout the US over a three-year period. I felt that this same method could work for my coaching business because the other methods I had tried were not working.

I began calling CEOs to coach them specifically. I found that they were difficult to reach. Some answered, most did not. Some were open for appointments, most were not. Often their executive assistant would transfer my call to human resources. Sometimes I got a call back for an appointment, mostly not. Since I had the other executives on my company profile sheets I would simply start calling down the list and leave messages. If I was unable to reach the CEO after many attempts, I could call down the list and potentially work with another executive in the company. After 1,000 calls, I had developed a foundation for my business with one CEO client and three VPs. Not bad. I know it sounds like a lot of calls, but it is a very low-cost way to set up appointments, meet people face to face, and launch a business.

Cold Call Story: After a recent cold call to a CEO of a large company, I received this message from her assistant, "Hi Donna, this is Katie [executive assistant] from Chris's [CEO] office at ABC [Company]. You had called last Friday, and I've had a chance to touch base with Chris and also she received your lovely note yesterday. All the executive coaching and consulting goes through our HR department and I was able to talk to our VP of HR and let her know that I am forwarding your information, which I just did, so you should be expecting a call from our HR department. Again, thanks so much for reaching out to us and somebody will be in touch. Bye now."

I called the CEO's executive assistant back to thank her for such a professional message. She also shared the name of the VP of HR, which is listed on their website, but it was helpful to know who exactly she contacted to share my information.

A few weeks later, I received a call from the VP of HR. We scheduled a meeting, even though she said they already have executive coaching in place. I pointed out that often companies will have a portfolio of coaches. She agreed to meet with me which is the goal you are going for on calls: to make an in-person appointment with a decision maker.

True, it is a lot of work to cold call and stay organized and optimistic. You have daily call tracking for data analysis, research and follow up. All of that is worth the effort to be independent where you can stay at home with your children and set your own schedule. In addition to that, you are doing meaningful work. I found I was much happier selling my professional coaching than a product I was not as passionate about. The entire summer when I was building my executive coaching business, I limited my work hours to strictly cold call for two hours a day. I did this in the early morning while my kids were sleeping. Then I was able to spend the rest of the day enjoying time with my children.

When you have the freedom to attend your child's soccer game, take them to the pool, have their friends over, cook dinner together, play board games, read books together, and as a bonus, impact people's lives profoundly through your work, you have time freedom and meaningful work! You feel fulfilled, flexible, and free! I had this much flexibility when I ran my own business from home and you can too. I did not have that kind of flexibility working in a corporate job – even when I worked part time from home – because I still had to go into the office several days a week. Having the freedom to work from home and spend more time with my children became my sole goal in life. I was willing to do what it took to conquer my fears because I desperately needed to be available to my children on my own terms.

After you plant seeds by contacting people who need your coaching services, nurture those seeds by developing relationships. Eventually you will get to reap the harvest by closing business and working with clients. When the money starts coming in from your business development efforts, it is a great feeling to know you can support your family. Now you have both time freedom and financial freedom!

When you see the impact your coaching has on another person's life and hear them tell you how you have changed their life, you want to dance for joy! You have arrived. You are doing what you love to do. You are being paid well to do this work and your clients appreciate what you do for them. The best part is that you are delighted to be a role model for your children as a happy parent. You can design your work schedule around your passions and family priorities. Life doesn't get much better than that for a working parent! Ideally you can choose to stay home when your kids are young and then work from home when your children enroll in school.

What can I advise you to do if you are like most people and do not enjoy cold calling? There are other ways to build a business. Some I have tried. Other ways have not worked as well for me, most likely because it was not fun for me or too time consuming, costly, or diffi-cult. That doesn't mean you cannot try them. Do anything that you are comfortable with to let people know you are in business and able to help them. Try one marketing method with gusto for an entire year. I suggest you try cold calling or something more frightening like public speaking or less frightening like writing. Know who you are and stretch yourself. If you are slightly uncomfortable, good, that means you are learning.

Even now that I have moved for the third time to a new state since I began my coaching business, my plan is to cold call in the largest city in my state and the largest cities that are one flight away from my city. Even though I rely mainly on cold calling, I also speak, write, utilize social media, webinars, and podcasts.

Looking back at all the various marketing and advertising options, cold calling stands out as the main way that worked for me in building my business on practically a zero budget.

When we moved to California, I secured ongoing business with my CEO client and decided I could build my business anywhere having built my business in the small college town of Oxford, Ohio by focusing my efforts on the larger metropolitan city of Cincin-nati. I proceeded the same way as before, researching local businesses through library databases and setting up a cold calling campaign.

New Mexico is not like other states I have lived. There are not a lot of company headquarters to call on. Even though New Mexico is challenging, I have started working with some local clients through an ad in the local paper and online. I am continuing my cold calling campaign to determine needs in the local area as well as several South-west states as I build my global online presence.

If you find yourself in a similar geographical quandary, what can you do? This work does not necessarily require you to be in person. I know many coaches whose entire business is by phone and therefore it makes no difference where they live. You have the option of phone, videoconference, or face to face. You can be sensitive to your client's needs and be flexible in your delivery methods. All coaching delivery methods are effective, and each has its unique benefits. It truly is up to you and your client as to how you will proceed with each coaching session.

You will get discouraged at times and you might consider giving up and starting a different business. Warning! Do not lose sight of your passion. Stay on track. After many months of getting to know the local market and not landing enough new business to keep my executive coaching business growing, I found a business opportunity to sell private label products online. My hope was that I could create another stream of income which I did, but at a personal cost. The dramatic initial success afforded me a large business loan to grow the business, yet I found that I had abandoned my passion entirely and was running a business I am not passionate about. This was an expensive lesson. It was time to start coaching again.

Do not give up on your passion!

Your geography may be equally challenging, yet with either using the phone only or online video technology, you can coach anyone practically anywhere. Your clients may be willing to pay your travel expenses if they prefer in person appointments, or they may choose to travel to you. I enjoy in person coaching, this is my primary offering. I found cities that are just a flight away to cultivate business. I narrowed my target list, focusing on large businesses for a total of thirty companies until I had exhausted the list. Then I created a new list of thirty, and so on, until I had created a new foundation of solid clients.

Prospecting by cold calling is strictly a numbers game and nothing to be taken personally. The more you experiment, the better you do. Track your numbers and you will see how it works. You will have many "Nos" before a "Yes" and when you get a "Yes" you need to amp up your calling because you are feeling great and that feeling comes through to your prospects. People are attracted to people who are enthusiastic and have a passion for their work. If you need to practice feeling joyful, take that time out and practice. You have the power to feel ecstatic by connecting with joy in every moment. Create the proper mindset and positive emotional state before you start calling people. Spread the joy!

Cold calling is not easy. Most would say that this is the most difficult way to build a business. I disagree because I tried other methods and cold calling was the most direct, least costly, and most effective way for me. How many companies have sales forces that do the same thing? Every company I have ever worked! How many coaches are cold calling? Very few. I was in a room of about 500 coaches and the speaker asked the audience, "Who enjoys cold calling?" I was the only person in the audience to raise my hand. It was kind of embarrassing and I thought maybe I wasn't being honest with myself. But, the reason I raised my hand was because I love the results of cold calling. I have experienced a very successful executive coaching business as a result of cold calling. Why wouldn't I enjoy cold calling? True, there is a lot of rejection, but it is a numbers game and some people do need your help. You simply need to understand that and keep offering your help. Don't be stingy holding back your services. Be philanthropic in your campaign – people need what you have to offer! Once you make enough calls and see the numbers, you can see how this tried and true system works.

To build a sustainable business, you must have a consistent way of creating leads that translate to prospects that become clients. It is time consuming, but I found I could reach the people I needed to talk to more quickly by calling them directly than hoping they read my article, met me at a networking event, or came to my class. Large company CEOs were not showing up at these events anyway. The main thing I did right was to choose one method of marketing and stick with it for an entire year. Over time, I noticed that I had certain months of the year that I would cold call. That activity was enough to allow me to coast the rest of the year, enjoying the work with my coaching clients while balancing most of my time with my family. I generated enough leads and closed enough business during just a few months a year when I focused hard on calling and tracking my numbers.

There are more effective targeted ways to reach your clients with your messaging that casts a net in a sea of people ready and eager to hear your messages and learn from you. Many people are now using social media and building a community following through their email list. By providing free content that leads to paid programs working with other list builders to market to multiple lists at the same time, you can build your community quickly. The effort is in maintaining that communication by preloading content each month, so that the system works behind the scenes while you focus on the most intriguing work coaching your clients.

I am currently experimenting with online content. It is not easy to keep up this effort without a system and an assistant who can run the campaigns for you. You cannot do it all, but in the beginning, you might need to until you have created plenty of business. Once you have secured enough business and your time is focused more on coaching, you can have your assistant run the marketing campaigns for you. If you have created an effective marketing funnel, you need to continually feed the community information and create a flow of leads into your funnel. Then you must have programs to sell to your community and a way to convert leads to prospects and prospects to clients.

Secure Clientele

Create a marketing funnel where you easily obtain leads that can be qualified as prospects to become clients. Leads often fit the demographic you are targeting and then you must qualify the lead to establish a prospect, a person interested in working with you, then you can close the prospect to create a client, someone who is ready and able to work with you now. Create connection with each lead or prospect and build a community by contacting them directly via email or phone. Continue to communicate with your prospects and close new business. Repeat this cycle continuously to sustain a constant flow of new clients. Make it fun, set goals, and celebrate successes!

You do not need a lot of client companies as an executive coach; three to five is a great number. If you can work with more, that is up to you, but this number worked for me and I was quite successful. You *do* need a marketing funnel that is continually providing leads and prospects to sustain your business. Profile your target market by determining your ideal client title, and their area of expertise, for example CEO, COO, VP operations, VP sales, VP human resources, size of business, industry, and gross revenues.

I targeted thirty companies to begin. I wanted to call on them consistently enough to be able to reach an ideal client. It takes *at least* seven contacts to get a call back. You must listen well for needs and demonstrate you can solve their problems to obtain an appointment. You want a manageable list to make the best use of your time.

What *not* to do: Allow me to reiterate this point. Do not make your target company list too large.

Prospecting Story: When I moved to Northern California, I created a huge database, thinking the more the merrier. I tried expanding my list, thinking I could grow it faster and purchased a license to a customer database to automate my cold calling process. Creating a large database made it overly challenging for one person to handle because the software program was more complex than I needed for my sole proprietorship. I hired a consultant to customize the software and teach me how to use it. I hired students to load company data into the client relationship management program. Expanding my list caused overwhelm and wasted resources. Having tried that, I found the first approach worked best, thirty companies at a time, with a manual system. I could spend focused time on a reasonable number, rather than try to tackle too many and only work with A, B and C named companies.

I advise you to find ways to reach your ideal clients that works for you and your lifestyle. If you can automate it easily, go for it. Stick to one marketing plan for a year to gain momentum to close business. With the internet, you have more ways to reach people through social media platforms such as Linked In, Facebook, Instagram, Twitter and more. With social media and your website, you can release free content via video clips, a blog, posting thoughts of the day, interesting relevant quotes, or inspirational stories. You can post articles and tips for effective leadership, executive presence, fulfillment at work, life balance, emotional intelligence, self-actualization, and any topics of interest to you and your clients. By communicating in various ways in an ideal avenue, you will start to develop a community where you can convert leads into prospects and begin closing business by selling your executive coaching program.

The ability to create new business is essential. Discover the best way for you to build your business and stick with this technique for an entire year. Track your statistics converting leads to prospects and prospects to clients. Refine your ability to close new business. Celebrate your success. The best feeling you can have as a coach is facilitating and observing a transformational outcome for your client. Your goal is to help your client discover their authentic leadership role, crystalize their mission and vision and actualize their true self. While you are serving your clients and company stakeholders remember to take care of yourself. *You* are a *key* stakeholder as well! Develop yourself! Practice treating yourself like royalty because you are an instru-

ment of growth and personal potential. Maintain self-care as you grow
your business.

Chapter 12:

Obstacles and How to Overcome Them

"So, who do you trust, fear or love? Fear tells you to hide your true self. Love tells you to stand up and shine. Fear wants perfection. Love is perfect despite appearances. Fear tells you being right is the way to stay safe. Love knows safety is an illusion. Fear argues for your limitations. Love takes a stand for your greatness."
– Author Unknown

Fear, doubt, and the Charlatan Complex are like weeds in the soil preventing your optimal growth. These weeds are holding you back from doing the work you love and offering your services to others.

Are you worried that you do not have enough credibility as a coach or as an executive to coach chief executive officers and high-level business leaders? Have people you respected put doubt in your mind about your profession or experience? Has your fear paralyzed you?

These are all fears that I have experienced. You will find reasons to doubt yourself as you step up to your own greatness. A common fear is "Am I good enough?" It is not easy to shake self-doubt. The best way to shake it is to go out and offer your services again and again. As you work with clients, you will gain experience and over time, you will become an expert.

Many can relate to the charlatan complex, or imposter syndrome: the feeling of not being good enough or getting away with pulling the wool over someone's eyes. I often had to pinch myself working with such accomplished leaders. I had to remind myself they are people too, complex human beings with human problems walking this unknown path.

Facing My Fears to Have a Vision

A Three-Day Solo in the Wild: My first experience camping by myself happened during a "Vision Fast" (similar to a Vision Quest) in 2004. I had spent the previous year studying and practicing meditation daily through my master's coursework at Naropa University. A wilderness course that summer compelled me to venture out with ten fellow students into the Wyoming desert. I had always dreamed of doing a vision quest and here was my opportunity to camp solo while fasting and perhaps have a "vision," a symbolic experience.

The first few nights we camped with the group and our guides as they prepared us for our solo experience. They taught us various pancultural traditions and rituals such as a death lodge that we would perform on our own during our solo experience. The fourth night we each spread out far enough from base camp to feel alone, but still close enough to see each other and be able to head back to base camp if need be. I remember finding my spot, noticing the dark night and the feeling of fear rising in my body. I knew that my mind was making up stories. I was able to tame my thoughts and focus on the present.

I put my backpack and sleeping bag down. I prepared the area where I was going to sleep by laying down my thin air mattress and then I pulled out my sleeping bag, my navy blue Ajungulak. I felt as though I was greeting an old friend I had not seen in years. I had spent night after night with that same backpack and sleeping bag in 1985 traveling around Europe on my own for almost six months. Here I was again, on my own.

I slipped inside my bag and felt the comfort of Mother Earth supporting me from below. Hundreds of miles away from city lights, I looked up to the overwhelming beauty of layers upon layers upon layers of stars, feeling comforted under the blanket of Father Sky. I was home.

That night as I laid awake, I watched multiple shooting stars until my eyelids were too heavy to remain open. The crickets sang a song as I drifted off to sleep. I saw a vision in my mind of Mother Earth and Father Sky transcending my parents' role. Trust the universe. I woke up to a sweet chipmunk's chirp darting around me and looked up to a smiling moon. Soon I heard the drumbeat from base camp signaling us to return to the group.

The next day, we each hiked many hours to choose our individual camp spots. Mine was in a beautiful sand castle area with large sandstones near a wooded area. I first came across a caterpillar and then a butterfly, reminding me of my first website where I was inspired by transformation and used the quote, "Just when the caterpillar thinks the world is over, she becomes a butterfly."

That night after preparing my sleeping area, I walked up to sit on a ledge to view the sunset. There in the distance, in front of the bright orange ball, stood a black stallion. The horse whinnied and stomped its hoof in my direction. In my mind's ear, I heard, "Come on!" The horse stood there a long time and then paced back and forth turned and looked my way again. I wondered about this message as I gazed at the setting sun.

I felt a presence nearby and looked slightly to my left. I was staring at the eyes of a wild animal just ten feet away. A mountain lion! I had heard our guide tell a story about a mountain lion who had visited one of the campers in the same northeast area I had chosen. My body went into a state of frozen panic. My heart started pounding in my chest like a bass drum: boom, boom, boom. I told myself to breathe slowly, knowing that animals can sense fear. I sat perfectly still staring eye-to-eye with the mountain lion. Minutes went by as I worried I could be attacked and killed by this wild animal.

My eyes slowly adjusted to the dark night. The bright orange ball that lingered in my vision slowly disappeared and I found myself staring into the eyes of a deer – a deer – just a deer! I had imagined I was staring down a fierce animal. Because my eyes had been blinded by the sunset, I missed out on a friendly gaze of a deer and a potential telepathic message. I believe the spirit of the deer represented my mother whereas the horse represented my father. That night was the night I had prepared a death lodge ceremony calling on my deceased parents and grandparents for support in a ritual I had been preparing for all day long. I looked over at the horse again and watched it trot off into the sunset. Such a beautiful sight!

What profound beauty I was fortunate to experience living in and with nature. It is wonderful to be in the wild amongst the sun, stars, moon, and animals and experience a universal sense of home.

Lesson Learned in the Wild

It is interesting how the mind can make up the scariest version of reality. This can happen in business as well. You may think you are about to meet with a lion and find out the lion is a deer. You could have spent that panic time enjoying the moment, knowing there was nothing to fear at all.

Do not allow fear to get in your way. The best way to handle this is by learning to observe your mind and tame your thoughts. Once we allow ourselves to let go of our stories, we can remain present in the moment and respond mindfully, centered in the present moment, with what is in fact happening.

Meeting the Lion Face to Face in Business: After several phone conversations, I set up a meeting with a prospect I felt confident in closing. This was one of my first meetings with a chief executive officer of a large company, after blowing the sales process during a previous meeting with a chief executive officer of another local company. I was determined to be fully prepared this time. I decided to dress for success, wearing my favorite suit to look my best and feel confident. I was ready to move through this fear and close the business.

I carefully prepared my proposal, had my best notebook and pen, and showed up to the appointment thirty minutes early. I decided to sit in my car preparing mentally and emotionally for this meeting. I noticed the anxiety and fear rising as I antici-pated meeting this man who held a position of power and per-haps my fate as an executive coach. With my body full of nerves, I focused my mind on my breath, first noticing the breath as it was. I focused on the feeling of the breath as it entered my nose and exited my nose. Any time my mind wandered to the future, or the past, I pulled it back to the breath to focus on the present moment. I paid attention only to my breath to calm the body. In this way, I was able to bring my mind into the present moment fully.

Once my body was in a very calm state, I began to rehearse the meeting from the start all the way to the point of my prospective client signing the agreement I had prepared. Having faced the image of the mountain lion, I knew I could get through this meeting alive.

As the CEO signed my agreement, I felt a sense of accomplishment. I had moved through fear to enjoy the thrill of success.

You may doubt your abilities even though you have learned coaching skills and have worked as a coach for some time honing those skills. You know that logically you can coach anyone, but you are unfamiliar with what a chief executive officer might need.

How do you move forward and work with fear and doubt?

One way to work with fear and doubt is to realize that they are not real. These are stories that your mind is making up to keep you in the safety zone. It is threatening to the ego to go out on a limb and potentially humiliate oneself. Your mind creates a story of the worst-case scenario to keep you from changing. Change is scary and sets you up for potential failure, which the ego is working to protect you from. Yet, change also sets you up for achieving greatness and in that case, the ego must be tamed. Tell the ego you will be okay in this situation and it can take a rest.

You must create a compelling vision for your future to move through and conquer your fear. It is helpful to create a vision statement of the person you are becoming and read this statement to yourself out loud every day, even twice a day if possible. Your subconscious mind will accept the vision statement describing the person you are becoming and get to work assisting you to become that person. Even as you sleep, the subconscious mind will be working on solutions to set you up for success.

How to Create a Vision Statement

1. Write down what goal you wish to achieve. Let's use the example of $100K in revenue by the end of this year. Write a specific amount by a specific date. Stretch yourself and be ready to put an actual plan in place to meet the goal.

2. Write down what you intend to offer in return. For example, "I will serve ten ideal clients by providing executive coaching."

3. Write your statement in the present tense as if it is already happening. For example, "I serve ten ideal clients by providing executive coaching."

4. Feel the emotion you will feel when you are living in that reality.

5. Copy this statement on several pieces of paper and place these vision statements in areas around your office and home where you will likely read them often.

6. Feeling the emotion of joy and success, read the statements aloud twice a day.

By reading the statements aloud, twice a day, you are programming the mind to believe that you are already successful. You are changing every day into the person you visualize you can be. Your subconscious mind is helping you get there by focusing on what you want to become and helping you navigate your way.

Keep your client testimonials on a vision board so that you can remind yourself how you make clients feel, what their story was when you met them and what their story became through the work you did together.

Here are some of my client testimonials, "Donna's consistent professionalism let me know I would be 'safe' in talking with her…she has very strong listening skills." "I trusted Donna immediately, she not only provided great direction, she guided me through some major changes in both my professional and personal life. I am much more self-aware." "Donna helped increase my self-awareness with the 360 and helps shed light on people's opportunities for improvement without ruffling feathers ... she is very perceptive and makes a quick read on a person." "I think you are a magician! The change you drove in our executive was incredible." "The work you do is greatly needed, consider me a champion!" "Now I can die happy knowing that I pursued my dream. You saved my life. I have been planning this business for twenty-two years, twenty-two years! Now it is becoming a real business. I am a totally different person! I feel twenty years younger! I feel like myself again!"

I have these client reminders to keep me from wallowing in self-doubt or feeling like a charlatan when I am facing a new opportunity. When you are the product, you must do a lot of internal work to boost your emotional state so that you can boldly walk this path. You are making an impact on people's lives, helping them become true to themselves, more integrated, whole, and happier. This is valuable work and sometimes you will forget that and get in your own way by allowing yourself to get distracted so that you can stay safe. But, leadership is not safe, it is stepping to your edge continuously to make an impact in the world.

If leadership was easy, everyone would be a leader. Most people do not want to lead which is why so many people are suffering. They need you, they need your leadership! Taking a stand for humanity is a tough job. Yet, you would not be resonating with the work as a coach if you were not meant to take a leadership role in life. Because you have found your calling as a coach, you must persist and plow through the self-doubt. Stop playing it safe–staying in your cocoon–and get out there and serve.

I work with entrepreneurs as well, and recently had a client tell me through tears, that she was going to have a heart attack if she stayed in the current role she was in. She acknowledged me and my work telling me that I saved her life! She would die happy! That was difficult for me to take in and truly believe, but when she repeated the same thing on a future visit, it sunk in. This work *is* life-saving. She avoided having a heart attack from stress or taking prescription drugs just to cope in her abusive work environment. Instead, she took action and hired me to coach her to take the leap of faith and pursue her passion. She was finally able to take the risk to follow her calling with my support and encouragement. She is deeply grateful that I gave her the go ahead to follow her dream and make it a reality.

Sometimes all people need is the permission to honor their dreams, their calling, and their vision for their life. I work with my client's wisdom and you will too. You do not have to have all the answers, because your client has wisdom for their direction. You just need to draw out those answers by using your curiosity, intuition, and inquiry. Be careful not to over prepare and instead be present to listen to your client's wisdom.

It is exciting to see a client's whole demeanor transform and confidently shine walking a clear path. I cannot think of any work more important than this. This is my calling and it is your calling too! Stick with it because the rewards are great. It is an honor to be a catalyst for another human being as they become the person they have dreamed they could be.

Every day, you must decide if you are willing to step up to the call and put yourself out there in the world to be of service. Are you willing to do what it takes to be that support person for someone else transforming from the caterpillar state to the butterfly? Are you willing to help them through this growth period that is both uncomfortable, scary, and exciting all at the same time?

Your vision will draw you through the obstacles. My vision is a world of happy and whole people releasing their natural gifts and talents with the world. What is your vision?

Celebrating Success

When you do experience successes, either through your sales process (such as meeting a prospective client and having this client sign your agreement), or your coaching process (hearing your client tell you that you have changed their life profoundly), it is time to celebrate. Mark this moment and your achievement by treating yourself with something that honors your values of health, family or fun, for example.

Dealing with the Charlatan Complex

There were, and still are, many days I suffer from the charlatan complex, feeling as though this work is not valuable. "Anyone could do this! Should I be charging this much for my services when this work feels like play at times? I mean, I am only doing what I love to do. How hard is it to ask obvious questions? Just stay home today. No need to risk going out into the world. Nobody cares what you have to offer."

Who is that talking? It certainly is not my higher self, who knows how important this work is. It is my ego, working its dark magic to keep me safe.

You may be saying similar negative comments to yourself. You must catch these thoughts and discard them. You must stand up to your own ego and let it know who is boss here. You know better than to listen to these limiting thoughts.

Think about it logically. Do you want to live a safe life? Do you want to hide out in your cocoon? Do you want to build up layers of that cocoon to the point you cannot escape? I doubt it – you wouldn't be reading this book. Hiding and playing small is safe but is also boring! You know deep down that you are a leader and can help bring people to the other side of life: this side of the river where life is excit-ing. On this side of life, people are doing great work and cannot wait to do more of it.

You have experienced the state of flow while working and know that this is available to you and to anyone who wants to step up to their own plate. You have chosen to truly live by stretching your potential and actualizing your true self. For you to truly live, that means working with others to help them achieve their dreams, live out their potential, and lead a meaningful life. This kind of work is priceless. You must take a stand and make an impact in the world.

How do you know your talent is valuable?

Notice When Clients Experience Breakthroughs

Here is a sample of some of my clients' breakthroughs. You will notice that some are personal, some professional, and some cross over into both areas of life. When you coach your clients, you are dealing with the whole person, therefore any work you do together will impact their whole life, not just their professional life.

Client one: receives a two-level promotion shortly after exploring her secret passion, *client two:* celebrates twenty year career with a joy-filled, tear-filled, moving ceremony full of staff and community member testimonials, *client three:* moves from zero self-awareness to being able to monitor his body language and emotional levels during an intense meeting with a previous adversary, *client four:* recommits to his faith and his wife by renewing their wedding vows, *client five:* turns around a multimillion dollar failing business unit to show a profit while regaining customer trust, *client six:* lands dream job within two weeks, meets the woman of his dreams, marries her within a year, and enrolls in a master's degree program in line with his passion, *client seven:* quits her job, attributes coaching to "saving her life" and starts a new business in her sixties, the business she dreamed about for over twenty years, *client eight:* tells his nine-year-old son he loves him for the first time, *client nine:* wrote a new poem after an eight month block and read it proudly to a live audience, *client ten:* increased self-awareness and lands a dream job that fits her need to be more present for her sons as a single mom and "adores" her new boss, *client eleven:* gains confidence to ask the board for $10M in funding and receives approval.

Ask Clients for Feedback

Quarterly at a minimum, provide your client a survey to fill out, or interview and record their feedback. From this feedback, you can ask for a testimonial you can provide in your marketing materials.

How Do You Know Your Mission Is Worthy?

Joy is a sign that you are on the right track. Notice how you feel helping others by supporting their dreams, drawing out their wisdom, expanding their conscious awareness, and witnessing their personal and professional growth. Consider the joy you feel when you are following your passion and cultivating your strengths, interests, and talents by developing yourself.

How Do You Keep Your Dream Alive?

To keep your dream alive, keep working with clients. This work feeds your soul. If you doubt your abilities, read client testimonials. Develop a marketing funnel. Teach a class, lead a workshop, write, and speak about your passions and your work.

Daily Practice

Develop a daily practice of sitting meditation or reflection. Do not judge yourself if you are unable to do this practice daily or forget somedays, just do your best. Even if you spend two minutes a day, that is all that is necessary. You may grow your practice to ten minutes, twenty minutes, or thirty minutes a day. You will find what works best for you; some days are different than other days and that is fine, no judgment. Do what it takes to nurture your own sense of self, developing that confidence to step out into the world with your message.

Here are samples of a daily practice:

- Brief Sitting Meditation, ten minutes

- Boil water for tea, sit in silence as water boils, focus the mind on the breath.
- Forty-five minutes – One Hour Moving Meditation
- Go for a mindful walk, noticing each foot print as you breathe in with one step and breathe out with the other step.
- Go for a swim, noticing the feeling of the water as you move through it.
- Practice yoga on your own or attend a group class. Stay focused on your breath as you start each expanding movement, such as lifting arms overhead, with the inhale and start each contracting movement, such as a forward fold, with the exhale.
- Ten minutes to thirty minutes sitting meditation either silent or may incorporate:
  - Recite Vision Statement
  - Read an inspirational passage from a book or a poem
  - Meditate
  - Recite Affirmations

Develop Confidence and Emotional Strength

1. Read client testimonials
2. Recite Affirmations
   Examples from my daily practice book:
   - "Today is a brand-new beautiful day. I am grateful to be alive. How will I make the most of today?"
   - "I am open to all the abundance in the Universe. I am grateful for everything I am experiencing. Thank you!"
   - "I think big, allowing myself to notice and accept all the good in life."
   - "I do my work with love. I enjoy working with my clients."
   - "I help others become happy, healthy, and free and in return, life supports me wonderfully."

- "I permit myself to be deserving of all the good I receive from life."
- "I live in a loving abundant universe and am deeply grateful for loving family friends and clients." (Name specific people in your life and bring their image and essence to mind feeling their loving support.)
- "I trust the universe to support me in my journey. I will proceed as way opens."
- "I am successful and prosper at every turn."
- "Unlimited prosperity is everywhere. I am open to receiving all that I need to do and all that I imagine I am capable of doing."
- "I love the freedom I feel with financial abundance."
- "At this very moment, enormous wealth and power are here for me and I am deserving."
- "I feel immense joy as I am able to visualize the end result, working with my ideal clients, doing great work in the world, releasing clients from negative emotions to positive emotions. I can see my crystal-clear vision expand in all its magnificent beauty."
- Create your vision board. Place it in your office where you can rest your eyes.

My vision board includes activities and people that inspire me. I enjoy gazing at a photo of a person swimming, riding a horse, riding a bike, skiing, running on the beach, dancing, doing yoga on the beach, speaking – these are motivating and validating of what I do and what I enjoy doing. Also, I enjoy seeing faces of family and mentors, reading words of inspiration, seeing healthy food I enjoy eating – validating my values and habits. I enjoy gazing at pictures of our family experiencing exotic places, and ideal homes where I can entertain family and friends, beach homes, pools, beaches, and beautiful places, like

Esalen, to remind me to take care of my spirit. I enjoy images of the Dalai Lama, Thich Nhat Hanh, Jesus, and other mentors, teachers, authors, and leaders that inspire me to be my best.

1. Find a coaching buddy or colleague. It was helpful to me to create a friendship with another coach who was several steps ahead of me. When I had fears or successes, I had a friend to call who understood this business.

2. Hire a coach or mentor. Find a coach you admire and share your goals. Let your coach know how you want to be coached, communicate clearly what you have found to work best for you. Do not be afraid to speak up and manage your coach, or find a new one, to get the results and gain the experience you desire.

The important thing is to develop your product, *you*, and lead by example. The more love and support you have in your life, the more available and present you will be with your clients. Believe in yourself and maintain your enthusiasm and passion for life. You have this precious life and can choose how you spend your time and how authentic you choose to be. What life can you imagine in your wildest fantasy? What is your dream come true?

<blockquote>
"Row, row, row your boat
Gently down the stream
Merrily, merrily, merrily, merrily
Life is but a dream"
</blockquote>

Dream big!

Chapter 13:

Conclusion – You've Got This!

"The most beautiful fate, the most wonderful good fortune that
can happen to any human being, is to be paid for doing that
which he passionately loves to do."
– Abraham Maslow

Keeping Your Dream Alive

I wrote this book for you because you knew you wanted to be an entrepreneur as a child and young adult. Yet, you didn't have anyone to guide you as an entrepreneur. You have felt lost and alone trying to navigate life to the best of your ability. You have struggled to find your true self and do meaningful work in the world. You long for guidance and a clear path. You want to know who you are at your core and acknowledge your natural born talents. You know you are special and here on this planet for a purpose. You long to find meaningful work. You cannot do anything less. When you work without meaning, you feel empty inside.

I know. I have been in your shoes. Your spirit, your soul, and your passion matter. You must take yourself seriously now and listen to your calling in life. Because you are reading this book, you were meant to hear this. You have all the permission in the world to follow your heart!

My intention is to inspire you to act on your passion which will lead you to your purpose and a fulfilling life! If you continue to feel joy doing this work, and I know you will, you can be sure you are on the right track. You can integrate your values and actions as a coach. You can experience wholeness. You can express your creativity and your intuition, and experience meaningful work. You can experience freedom: freedom of time, freedom of expression, and freedom of self. To become an authentic leader takes persistence, but it is worth the effort because otherwise you will always feel inauthentic doing work that does not bring you meaning, does not lead you to your purpose, and does not bring you fulfillment.

My goal for almost twenty years was to find meaningful work. Having lost my parents at age twenty-one, I learned that life is short. I did not want to waste time working at something that had little meaning to me. As a parent, my search for meaning escalated because I wanted to raise my children with a sense of hope. If I could not find and follow my passions, how were my children to find and follow their passions? Finding my purpose had become my mission. And in doing so, I found work that is full of meaning. I love to help others navigate life more easily by clarifying what is most important to them and what brings them joy, and by helping them manifest that which they envision for their life and work.

I found work that is full of meaning which led me to a fulfilling life. You can too. I was able to be the mother and role model I wanted to be. You can too.

I knew if I followed my passion my children would see this option for themselves and begin at an earlier age to notice their passions. Your children will too.

I wanted my children to attend the school of their choice, follow their passion, and become who they dreamed to be. They both did that and are living passion-filled lives. Our children are happy, and we are proud of the men they have become. I also wanted my husband to follow his heart and become a professor. He did that and is now tenured faculty. I am proud of us both for chasing our dreams. I succeeded in doing meaningful work with total flexibility and attended my children's soccer games, tennis matches, ski competitions, track competitions, plays, recognition ceremonies, parent meetings, and volunteered at school and sporting events. You can too.

By creating a business that you can operate from home, you can schedule your work around your children's schedule. You can be that parent you dreamed you could be, a parent involved in your children's lives. You can become the healthy version of you by integrating your life by doing work you love. You can support your family financially and emotionally. I did that as well and so can you. You simply and profoundly need to give yourself permission to follow your heart and live a life of your dreams. You can materialize what you visualize. Keep dreaming big. Keep offering what you know in your heart is your gift to the world. Some people won't realize you are handing them a golden ticket and some people *will*. You just need to keep offering your golden ticket often enough so that those that do understand what you are offering, hire *you*.

You need a vision, a mission, a plan, and action. Be persistent, believe in yourself, reach out to others as often as you can and do not get down. Remember that like Willy Wonka, you are handing out golden tickets, and those that are willing to receive the golden ticket you offer are going to be thrilled they hit the jackpot! Their lives will transform because of you.

Remember my client's tears of joy flowing down her cheeks claiming I saved her life? How she would have died of a heart attack had she not come to me for guidance? This *is* meaningful work even *more* than I imagined. This is the kind of work you can do too.

It is an honor to help someone recognize their passion to find their purpose by acknowledging their desires and listening to the voice of their higher self that resides inside them. By staying present, loving your client as you would your child, you can help your client hear their higher self's hopes and dreams. Listen to the soul and give your client permission to be their most authentic self.

I know you will have many success stories to tell as you transform your own life into the life you have imagined. Be of service and reap the rewards. You deserve it!

Cheers to your potential! I believe in you!

Further Reading

Hidden Wholeness by Parker Palmer

A Way of Being by Carl Rogers

The Farther Reaches of Human Nature by Abraham Maslow

Emotional Intelligence by Daniel Goleman

Search Inside Yourself by Chade-Mang Tan and Daniel Goleman

Leading through Conflict by Mark Gerzon

The Secret Handshake by Kathleen Kelly Reardon

The 7 Habits of Highly Effective People by Stephen R. Covey

The Speed of Trust by Stephen M. R. Covey

Co-Active Coaching by Laura Whitworth and Henry Kinsey-House

Parenting with Love and Logic by Foster Cline and Jim Fay

PEAK: How Maslow Got His Mojo by Chip Conley

What Got You Here Won't Get You There by Marshall Goldsmith

Peace is Every Step by Thich Nhat Hanh

The Alchemist by Paulo Coelho

Presence by Peter M. Senge, C. Otto Scharmer, Joseph Jaworski, and Betty Sue Flowers
Servant Leadership by Robert Greenleaf
True North by Bill George
Power Listening by Bernard T. Ferrari

Acknowledgments

"Good leaders must first become good servants."
— Robert K. Greenleaf

I want to thank my family, friends, teachers, and mentors. Thank you, Rob, for suggesting I take a counseling course; I, just like my clients, needed the permission to do what I imagined myself doing. No matter what, you are always there supporting me and my dreams. I love riding the journey of life with you! Thank you, Ty and Cole, for being such awesome sons, interesting, kind, fun, and funny! What a gift to observe you both become independent, thoughtful, responsible young men living out your dreams. You truly changed my life and are such a pleasure to be with. You paid attention to your passions and made wise decisions.

I want to acknowledge my loving parents, Dotty (Phillips Jones) and Bill Jones (Dr. William S. Jones), for being such strong, wise, and loving role models in my life. Mom and Dad were the ultimate servant leaders. I am fortunate to have been raised in an ideal loving family environment with David and Diane. We each have so much to be grateful for, especially our beautiful families.

Thank you, Rey, for showing up at the right moments around campus inspiring me with your Native American wisdom. Thank you, Victoria, for adamantly pointing me to my first coaching course. Thank you, Debra Benton, for an inspiring speech and showing me your courageous spirit. Thank you, Bob Parsanko, for being a mentor and a friend, encouraging me in my role as an executive coach and consultant. Thank you, Chogyam Trungpa Rinpoche, for founding Naropa. Thank you, Thich Nhat Hanh, the Dalai Lama and Pema Chodron for your inspiring work.

Thank you, John Davis, for your enthusiastic encouragement to Naropa University's MATP program. Thank you, Susan Skjei, for your leadership in the authentic leadership program. Thank you to all the faculty in the transpersonal psychology program at Naropa University that supported my deep inner journey. I have never felt more supported and loved in an environment of healers and teachers. Thank you, John Bowers, for being such a caring and wise leader on our vision fast and sharing your sacred talking stick with me.

To the Morgan James Publishing team: Special thanks to David Hancock, CEO & Founder for believing in me and my message. To my Author Relations Manager, Bonnie Rauch, thanks for making the process seamless and easy. Many more thanks to everyone else, but especially Jim Howard, Bethany Marshall, and Nickcole Watkins.

Thank you to every client for trusting me and allowing me to draw out your passion and potential. It is an honor to be a part of your journey. Thank you to my family Rob, Ty, Cole, David, Dawn, Diane and Eric, and all my nieces and nephews for all of your love.

Thank you, Erin and Jim Cencula, Monika Ludin, Holly Oberoi, Lex and Rachel Sumi, Tim and Terri Leiter, Chris and Jennifer Todd, Dave Karan, and Roberta Tolan, for your loving friendship for all these years.

Thank You

Thank you for reading Passion Purpose Profit! I am excited that you are exploring ways to be more available to your children and do meaningful work. Your children need you! Your past business experience, parenting experience and coaching education have set you up for coaching leaders. Leaders need your support and will appreciate what you offer. I trust that you will gain fulfilment by being of service to others. I hope you are encouraged to start your home-based authentic executive coaching business.

Please visit my website www.karabaconsulting.com/toolkit to download helpful tools to support your Authentic Leadership Business Model™ as you build your new business.

FREE TOOLKIT:

For a collection of client tools to aid the Authentic Leadership Business Model™ and coaching practice visit www.karabaconsulting.com/clientforms or email donna@karabaconsulting.com

FREE VIDEO CLASS:

For a Passion Purpose Profit video class visit www.karabaconsulting. com/learninglibrary

If you are ready for a deeper dive, apply here www.karabaconsulting. com/apply and schedule a strategy session.

Cheers to leading a balanced and fulfilling life!

Donna Karaba

About the Author

Donna Karaba has been professionally developing leaders since 2003. From a Fortune 500 background, Donna was called to the field of professional coaching. She built an executive coaching business focused on CEOs and created The Authentic Leadership Business Model™ to share her methods with other coaches and business leaders. Donna develops leaders to be real, self-actualized whole human beings.

Donna stoked her soul's fire by starting a business that supports human potential at work. This flexible business enabled her to be the mother and leader she dreamed to be. Donna found the balance she craved to raise her children on her own terms while doing meaningful work that would also enable her family to pursue their passions.

Donna earned a master's degree from Naropa University in transpersonal psychology along with certificates from the Coaches Training Institute and Naropa's Authentic Leadership Program. Donna is also a Myers Briggs MBTI˚ Certified Practitioner and certified to deliver 360-degree assessment feedback through The Center for Creative Leadership and The Hay Group. Her clients have experienced powerful personal and professional transformation. Her vision is a world of happy people each following their passions.

Donna lives with her loving husband and soulmate Rob in Santa Fe, NM. Donna is the proud mother of Ty and Cole, two uniquely inspiring young men. Donna continues to chase her passion: living on purpose while encouraging others to pursue their passions.

Website: www.KarabaConsulting.com

Email: donna@karabaconsulting.com

Linked In: www.linkedin.com/company/KarabaConsulting

Facebook: www.facebook.com/KarabaConsulting

Twitter: www.twitter.com/donnakaraba

Instagram: www.instagram.com/donnakaraba